AF653739

GANDHI AND HIS RELIGION

Gandhian Studies for Peace and Research Series

1. Gandhian Model of Development and World Peace/*R.P. Misra*
2. Conflict Resolution Through Non-Violence : Role of the Universities, Vol. I : Science and Ethics
K.D. Gangrade and *R.P. Misra*
3. Conflict Resolution Through Non-Violence : Role of the Universities, Vol. II : Development Without Destruction
K.D. Gangrade and *R.P. Misra*
4. The Social Philosophy of Mahatma Gandhi/*K.S. Bharathi*
5. Gandhian Humanism/*Mohit Chakrabarty*
6. Gandhian Holistic Economics/*Shashi Prabha Sharma*
7. Ghandhian Spiritualism : A quest for the Essence of Excellence
Mohit Chakrabarty
8. Gandhian Perspective on Population and Development
A.K. Sharma
9. Thoughts of Gandhi and Vinoba : A Comparative Study
K.S. Bharathi
10. Economic Philosophy of Mahatma Gandhi/*Shanti Swarup Gupta*
11. The Political Thoughts of Mahatma Gandhi/*K.S. Bharathi*
12. Gandhi and 21st Century/*Janardan Pandey* (Ed.)
13. Gandhian Philosophy of the Spinning Wheel/*Mohit Chakrabarty*
14. Gandhian Satyagraha : An Analytical and Critical Approach
Ajay Shanker Rai
15. Gandhi and His Religion/*P.A. Raju*

About the Author

Dr. (Lt. Col.) Poosapati A. Raju commissioned on 02 February, 1964. Before commissioned, he obtained two Post Graduate Degrees : M. A. in Political Science and M. A. in Public Administration in the years 1958 and 1960 from Nagpur University. After joining Army Education Corps he secured M. Ed. in 1974 from Poona University. In 1982 he was awarded Ph. D. Degree in Political Science from Aurangabad University.

His first book : *Social and Political Ideas of Kandukuri Veeresalingam* (a study in political thought) a renaissance writer in later half of nineteenth century in Andhra Pradesh was published in 1986.

Presently he is editing his short stories : 'An Enquiry Into Spirit',

At present he is the President of Shobha Memorial Degree College, Jami, District Vizianagaram, Andhra Pradesh.

Gandhian Studies for Peace and Research Series-15

GANDHI AND HIS RELIGION

DR. (LT. COL.) P.A. RAJU
Founder President and Principal
Shobha Memorial Junior College
Jami, Vizianagaram Dist., Andhra Pradesh

CONCEPT PUBLISHING COMPANY, NEW DELHI-110059

All rights reserved. No part of this work may be reproduced, stored in a retrieval system, or transmitted in any form or by any means, electronic, mechanical, photocopying, recording or otherwise, without the prior written permission of the copyright owner and the publisher.

ISBN 81-7022-777-1

First Published 2000

© P.A. **Raju** (*b.* 1935)

Published and Printed by
Ashok Kumar Mittal
Concept Publishing Company
A/15-16, Commercial Block, Mohan Garden
New Delhi 110059 (India)

Phones: 5648039,5649024
Fax: 091–(11)–5648053
E-mail : publishing@conceptpub.com

In fond memory of my mother
ANNAPURNA
Whose prayers made me
What I am

PREFACE

GANDHI was like the Himalayas. One can see his magnificence from numerous view points. Today Gandhi is relevant and will remain relevant in future. Keeping this in view. I have tried to analyse his ideas on religion. In this realm there is hardly any research. His admirers and masses failed to see an atheistic streak in him. It is because of his radiance emitted from him, they missed this reality. From the lenses of social sciences if viewed, rationalist in him is found. He was a man of action. He had hardly any time for theoretical discussions. An atheist like Gora and an agnoistic like Jawaharlal Nehru his chosen heir were associated with him in action but not in thought. In reverse Gandhi admired Gora calling himself a 'super atheist' and he did not hesitate to declare that this country will remain safe in the hands of Jawaharlal Nehru. The meeting ground was action, aim and purpose in the context of making India a strong unified nation.

Gandhi never believed in any denominational religion. He found his religion in the heart of man. Unity of religions was the favourite theme of the Mahatma. He made the man the centre of every thing. In his programme of action, man became the ultimate measure of all things. When heart rules the man the divinity in him oozes out bringing succour to the weak and the meek. What this divinity is ? It is the good in man. In India, both her soil and her people seeped in and lulled by religion, need theistic language and idiom to comprehend secular principles. Gandhi could reach the masses with his impeachable theistic word and phrase. Hence secular ideas were neatly wrapped and aesthetically designed packets producing decor to theology and presented to the masses. The Western press dubbed this phenomenon in Gandhi as 'God Stunt'. Gandhi's aim was to remove evil in man and to strengthen the moral fibre in him. He wanted heart to take priority over mind. His religion lies in ethics. He was a Hindu. It is not the ritual and rite of Hinduism touched him. The higher realms of philosophy embedded in the *Upanishads* and the *Vedas* caught his imagination. Gandhian theology if at all there is one, it aims at selfless service and self realisation. As a practical individual his plan of action to this end was carefully textured by him. If it is followed, the individual will be on the trail of Gandhian ideology of selfless service and self realisation. With the progress of realising divinity in self he will become a better Hindu if he is a Hindu, a better Muslim if he is a Muslim, and a better Christian if he is a Christian. In short he will become a better individual. For the first time in the realms of theology God an imperceptible concept concretised identifying Truth with God or *vice versa*. Gandhi could feel the mysterious power in the march of this universe to a certain predetermined destination. He felt the mysterious power but did not spell out what the predetermined destination of this universe. He simply said it is 'Godward'. Because of this mysterious power, creation and life persist amidst destruction and death. The pangs of new life can be reduced if possible can be eliminated fully only when nonviolence becomes the carrier of growth of the individual from one stage to the other in his ceaseless march towards truth. Transformation of society from one stage to the other becomes painless. Revolutions will be there. At the same time societies need not get stained with blood.

Gandhi was anything but a mystic. His selflessness and self realisation brought him to the door step of mysticism. But he never attempted to enter into it nor interested in mystic ways of life. He was fit to be a mystic. But mystic hue never touched him. His abilities were aimed at in the service of mankind. He never tried for self salvation to have communion with that mysterious force which he felt. This mysterious energy has a purpose. It is to drive the universe from one stage to the other effecting the growth of man who is now at the periphery of truth. The aim of Gandhi was to make the individual march in step with the universe in its development, rather than making the individual remain aloof from his environment for self salvation. Gandhi's aim was to make the individual recognise divinity in himself and stir it. Consequently the evil in him will get subdued. And can take knocks with a smile to drive the evil out in his opponent. Gandhi reached to stage of Mahatma not through religion and God devotion but through the path of higher realms of Hindu philosophy embedded in the *Upanishads*, scriptures and epics.

He appeared before the masses with a concrete plan of elevating them from misery. They in turn titled him as Mahatma—the great soul. It became the orb to his name.

Life has two parts : Known and unknown. Though Gandhi was curious of the mysterious power behind the movement of the universe the unknown part of human life never fascinated him. As a social engineer his aim was to remove venom in man. He pleaded forcefully and worked relentlessly to improve the inputs in man to make him fit to work through heart and get delinked him from materialism. His scheme is towards the confluence of 'Deva' and 'Adeva' a serene deep blue waters with the fast gushing and roaring muddy waters that takes place. Gandhian religion is ethics. It steels the moral fibre in the individual. Life to him is no longer 'fragile and fugitive'. Gandhi gave armour to man. Denied sword which is always associated with religion. Gandhi was liberal. He was primarily an utilitarian when he approached the poor. But he was never a hedonist. He used religion to drive home his point. Beyond that religion has no use for him. He was nonconformist, a rebel in the cause of *Satyagraha* and nonviolence and a freedom fighter. In his ethos of nonviolence one finds in him an architect and a social engineer rolled into one to bring harmony in society and to effect painless and bloodless revolution in society in its onwards march to Godwards.

DR. (LT. COL.) P.A. RAJU

ACKNOWLEDGEMENTS

I am grateful to the authorities of the Institute of Gandhian thought and Peace Studies of Allahabad University, who allowed me to use the Institute's Library while I was at Allahabad.

I am grateful to my wife Mrs. Satyavathi Poosapati who from the beginning helped me in writing this book. She suffered long durations of silence while I was engaged in collecting, sifting collating material and writing. Very often I wonder had she not been active and infusing strength into me at moments of my weakness. I could not have completed this work.

DR. (LT. COL.) P.A. RAJU

CONTENTS

3

Gandhi and God, Prayer, Faith and All That

[illegible] prayer, faith and other words [illegible] kind were used to convey [illegible] meaning like the word [illegible] employed by Gandhi to [illegible] social phenomenon [illegible] device means to bring [illegible] change in society and man [illegible] these words have therefore [illegible] distinct meaning when [illegible] Gandhi has used these. But [illegible] words are utilized in such [illegible] that the theistic content and [illegible] dominate more than the [illegible] meaning and the secular [illegible] therefore, necessary [illegible] the thick coat over them [illegible] show the secular content [illegible] different. And then only [illegible] employed and the [illegible] will be clear.

[illegible] is God? A hackneyed question. Any answer is hackneyed. [illegible] used very often words like God and religion. His critics and [illegible] called this phenomenon as "[illegible] saint". He did not use this [illegible]. But his readers and [illegible] were bewildered by his [illegible] asked numerous questions [illegible] numerous times. The result [illegible] had to perforce explain [illegible] meaning of these theological [illegible] to convey secular ideas [illegible] the theological mask [illegible] signals emanated. E[illegible] of theology became [illegible] powerful. Gandhi could [illegible] conveyed his secular concept [illegible] constraints of theology [illegible] him. The theological [illegible] consciously employed by him [illegible] achieve a definite purpose [illegible] not be uncovered. The lesser [illegible] could notice the rationalist [illegible] Gandhian writings. They [illegible] the bandwagon of people [illegible] Gandhi as a saint, even [illegible] Gandhi himself denied

1

INTRODUCTION

GANDHI was most popular during his days when he strode the Indian scene guiding and supervising the struggle for freedom. And today, his methods bring hope and infuse confidence in the suppressed and the weak yet he was misunderstood. Result is controversies. He is viewed as inconsistent and contradictory. Hence, there is debate about his relevance in the present context. Gandhi was primarily a rebel, a politician, a statesman and a revolutionary. And above all he is a thinker. His is an action oriented personality. He worked to bring succour to the poorest of the poor. In him all these rolled into one. Therefore, writing on Gandhi is a tough job. He is like the Himalayas. The magnificence of a view is different from different view points. Very often radiance that radiates may remain as a mask on realities. Identification and analysis of these realities will give an insight into Mahatmaji the great Soul.

Traversing to this reality is like voyaging across enchanted ocean. In the long voyage many things are surveyed. Beauty is appreciated and enjoyed. Peril in this voyage stimulates and inspires to adventure.

In India Gandhi is still a guide to many from a lay man to an articulated politician, from a liberal to a collectivist, and from a nationalist to an internationalist. Even an atheist like Gora and an agnoistic like Jawaharlal Nehru, his chosen successor who looked at him for guidance, sought blessings in their mission. Therefore in our country after laboriously discussing events of far reaching political and economic significance, conclusions are drawn only when these are viewed through the Gandhian lenses. Am I wiping out the tears from the eye of the poor? This makes the student as well as the scholar in Gandhian lore precise in examining and judging the flow of events.

Whenever Gandhi touched politics or economics, he appeared inconsistent. It was more apparent when he spoke on religion from his political pulpit or when he wrote in his *Young India* and *Harijan*. He himself wrote: "I would like to say to the diligent reader of my writings and to others who are interested in them that I am not at all concerned with appearing to be consistent. In my search after Truth I have discarded many ideas and learned many new things. Old as I am in age, I have no feeling that I have ceased to grow inwardly or that my growth will stop at the dissolution of the flesh what I am concerned with is my readiness to obey the call of Truth, my God, from moment to moment, and therefore, when anybody finds inconsistency between any two writings of mine, if he has still faith in my sanity, he would do well to choose the latter of the two on the same subject."[1] In the light of this Gandhi's ideas can be understood only when his ideas are separated and identified with historical events that had taken place on our march towards independence knocking out colonialism and in the liberation of man from fugitive existence towards progress. In these two aspects Gandhi was consistent like a machine. But in the realms of thought and philosophy he was inconsistent as he was in search of Truth. In his attempt to ameliorate the poor he remained always consistent. At no stage in any context he appeared inconsistent or contradictory.

In a different context, while commenting on *Varnashram Dharma* Gandhi wrote: "I have never made a fetish of consistency. I am a votary of Truth and I must say what I feel and think at a given moment on the question without regard to what I may have said before on it. It is for the reader to find out how far my present views coincide with those formerly expressed. Wherever he finds that what I have said or written before runs contrary to what I am writing now, he should without hesitation reject the former. As any vision gets clearer, my views must grow clearer with daily practice. Where I have deliberately altered an opinion, the change should be obvious, only a careful eye would notice a gradual and imperceptible evolution."[2] This shows his consistency to escort his audience in the dense jungle of the lore of various religions to a vantage point to see Truth which was God to him. Because of this aspect in Gandhi, Gora did not see any contradiction nor inconsistency in Gandhi. According to Gora Gandhi being "a man of non-violent creed these are stages of progress and not principle of contradiction."[3]

Gandhi's utterances on religion and theology at the surface seem to be contradictory. But his every concept has to be isolated in relation to other theological concepts and related to various events that prompted Gandhi to say these. Once a careful analysis is made a system and logic are found in Gandhi, what he wanted to teach the masses and the intellectual in the sphere of religion. Gandhi never analysed or discussed theology. The iron frame of religion superimposed on theology was removed. Therefore when it comes to religious aspect of Gandhi, one is not sure of what is visible as magnificent. The reality and magnificence get mixed up. Lay as well an intellectual may fall in ruts of thinking and fail to get the real meaning in the kernel of Gandhian ideas on religion. It is like a painting; one gets a broad sweep, yet important detail. The reality of the detail lies beneath the broad sweep. The reality of the detail has to be identified and interpreted. Interpretation of Gandhi should run parallel to the events of history. This would avoid the pitfalls of type cast that always stand on the way.

Gandhi removed the steel frame that generally encompasses theology and ethics. These were separated and presented as religion. He attracted two types of people. The first are swept by the current of Gandhian thought. They considered Gandhi was another Mahatma without the orb of God men like Ramana Maharishi. These kinds are Gandhites in conventional terminology. The second category are the critics of Gandhi. To them Gandhi was a revolutionary and touched every aspect of man to push the individual on to the road to progress. In this sphere of critical appreciation and analysis the critics of Gandhi find hidden wealth beneath his writings on religion, God and other concepts. Students of social sciences and religion studied his ideas thoroughly. Their conclusions on the surface appear divergent. But all these converge at a point where the uplifting of the poor comes in.

Words like religion, God, truth, faith etc., dominate discourses and deliberations of Gandhi. Concrete and subtleties have to be sifted. Gandhi used these words to emphasize and drive home a particular point at a specific event that made Gandhians get confused because of contradictions in statements and inconsistencies in his approach. The word religion with its connotation of dogma and creed obscures the meaning of the word *Dharma*. It has a different meaning in the Indian languages. Whenever Gandhi spoke about the word religion he had in mind the original meaning of *Dharma* as understood in Gujarati, his mother tongue. To him *Dharma* means relation with truth. It is a permanent element in man and finds full expression when man knows the maker and the self. Man becomes restless unless he finds himself in the Maker. In this context, the word Maker had nothing to do with the word 'God', but it is the universal self. Man's true fulfilment lies in realising the harmony between the self and the universal self. This is possible where truth and love prevail. At this stage not only the intellect alone but the heart is the requirement. It is because of the truth of the heart one feels he is free from anger and ill-will. His relations with his fellow beings and society at large remain smooth. Friction resulting into exploitation never takes place.

Transcending all religious creeds and sectarian ideas Gandhi said that God is Truth. And later modified this into 'Truth is God'. In the Gandhian lexicon, the words religion and God have different and distinct meanings. He gave a universalised as well as humanised meaning to the words God and religion.

Gandhi was the only leader in the struggle for freedom in our country who was a colossus. Before whom his contemporaries great in their own way and in their stature. He who was one of the few leaders understood the people and the country. He knew what the masses require and what idiom they comprehend. Accordingly he spoke. He was receptive. He worked for that social frame where friction is nill. At an early stage he understood the mood and temperament of his country and its people. He wrote: "India will never be Godless. Rank atheism cannot flourish in this land."[4] Because of this realisation Gandhi perforce took secular ideas and gave them a theological nomenclature. He clothed secular ideas with religious raiment. Therefore at every stage to convince the intellectual, the religious minded and the masses he gave statements often contradictory. To a very great extent he appeared inconsistent. But the aim and the path which he had chosen were clear to him. He was clear as far as the aim is concerned towards which the society has to be propelled. He was more clear about the path on which he had to bring society and the individual to realise the aim.

The word *dharma* if translated into ordinary social science terminology, meaning and aim of Gandhi will be clear. A purely

People like Gora and Bhagat Singh could call themselves atheists with a purpose, but not to ignore the divinity in man which makes him invincible. At this point Gandhi saw his Truth in atheists and they in turn found their aim coalesced with Gandhi's.

REFERENCES

1. *Harijan,* 29 April, 1933.
2. *Harijan,* 28 September, 1934.
3. Gora, *An Atheist with Gandhi,* Navajivan Publishing House, Ahmedabad, : 1951, p. 57
4. Gandhi, *Hind Swaraj*, Navajeevan Publishing House, Ahmedabad, Revised New Edition Reprint 1984, p. 92.
5. *Young India,* 30, August, 1928.
6. *Young India,* 29, May, 1924.
7. *Ibid.*
8. *Young India,* 28th August, 1928

so great. He had claimed to stand for truth and nothing less. But he has unconsciously misrepresented Jainism, Islam, Christianity and Hinduism itself. One having even cursory acquaintance with these faiths could easily discover the errors into which the great reformer strayed. He had tried to make narrow one of the most tolerant and liberal faiths on the face of the earth. And an iconoclast though he was, he has succeeded in enthroning idolatory in the subtlest form. He has idolised the letter of the *Vedas* and tried to prove the existence in the *Vedas* of every thing known to Science."[6]

When the Arya Samajists questioned about his biting criticism Gandhi wrote: "It was easy for me to suppress my opinion. But consistently without truth I could not do so when it became relevant. Hindu, Muslim tension is a grim reality. Removal of it is a stern national necessity. It cannot be brought about by ignoring or suppressing facts. Truth on such occasions must be told no matter how unpalatable it may be. But I claim no infallibility."[7] Gandhi was very clear about his aim and purpose. Amelioration of man took priority in his calculation over religious creed and faith. He was always consistent in his pursuit of his aim. The struggle for freedom gave him a wide platform to launch his movement where *Ahimsa* was the operating principle and *Sarvodaya* was the goal. Gandhi appreciated Brahmo Samaj for its liberalising and rationalising effect over Hinduism. He was critical towards Arya Samaj for erecting blocks between communities and paving way for communal disharmony.

In essence, to Gandhi "true religion is not narrow dogma. It is not external observance. It is faith in God, and living in the presence of God, it means faith in future life, in truth and in *Ahimsa*. There prevails today a sort of apathy towards these things of the spirit. Our temples appear today to be meant only for the simple and the ignorant. Few visit the real temples of God. Let the educated class take up the work of reform in this direction."[8]

Gandhi has to be studied from the point of view of his contribution in rationalising religion. In this endeavour a tenuous streak of atheism is discernible. The attempt is not to prove Gandhi as an atheist or to denigrate him, but to study certain aspects in Gandhi contrary to religion and theology. And how these help us to build a harmonious society.

People like Gora and Bhagat Singh could call themselves atheists with a purpose, but not to ignore the divinity in man which makes him invincible. At this point Gandhi saw his Truth in atheists and they in turn found their aim coalesced with Gandhi's.

REFERENCES

1. *Harijan,* 29 April, 1933.
2. *Harijan,* 28 September, 1934.
3. Gora, *An Atheist with Gandhi,* Navajivan Publishing House, Ahmedabad, : 1951, p. 57
4. Gandhi, *Hind Swaraj*, Navajeevan Publishing House, Ahmedabad, Revised New Edition Reprint 1984, p. 92.
5. *Young India,* 30, August, 1928.
6. *Young India,* 29, May, 1924.
7. *Ibid.*
8. *Young India,* 28th August, 1928.

so great. He had claimed to stand for truth and nothing less. But he has unconsciously misrepresented Jainism, Islam, Christianity and Hinduism itself. One having even cursory acquaintance with these faiths could easily discover the errors into which the great reformer strayed. He had tried to make narrow one of the most tolerant and liberal faiths on the face of the earth. And an iconoclast though he was, he has succeeded in enthroning idolatory in the subtlest form. He has idolised the letter of the *Vedas* and tried to prove the existence in the *Vedas* of every thing known to Science."[6]

When the Arya Samajists questioned about his biting criticism Gandhi wrote: "It was easy for me to suppress my opinion. But consistently without truth I could not do so when it became relevant. Hindu, Muslim tension is a grim reality. Removal of it is a stern national necessity. It cannot be brought about by ignoring or suppressing facts. Truth on such occasions must be told no matter how unpalatable it may be. But I claim no infallibility."[7] Gandhi was very clear about his aim and purpose. Amelioration of man took priority in his calculation over religious creed and faith. He was always consistent in his pursuit of his aim. The struggle for freedom gave him a wide platform to launch his movement where *Ahimsa* was the operating principle and *Sarvodaya* was the goal. Gandhi appreciated Brahmo Samaj for its liberalising and rationalising effect over Hinduism. He was critical towards Arya Samaj for erecting blocks between communities and paving way for communal disharmony.

In essence, to Gandhi "true religion is not narrow dogma. It is not external observance. It is faith in God, and living in the presence of God, it means faith in future life, in truth and in *Ahimsa*. There prevails today a sort of apathy towards these things of the spirit. Our temples appear today to be meant only for the simple and the ignorant. Few visit the real temples of God. Let the educated class take up the work of reform in this direction."[8]

Gandhi has to be studied from the point of view of his contribution in rationalising religion. In this endeavour a tenuous streak of atheism is discernible. The attempt is not to prove Gandhi as an atheist or to denigrate him, but to study certain aspects in Gandhi contrary to religion and theology. And how these help us to build a harmonious society.

peeped down deep into religious writings and searched what he wanted. At every stage he took the help of reason. He searched and thought about the aim of human life on this earth. He pondered over this enigmatic question; what is the aim of life? He searched religious lore for what he wanted. Raichand Bhai's writings dispelled doubts of Gandhi about Hinduism[14] Gandhi felt assured that Hinduism could give what he needed. Curiously at the same time Gandhi did not think of him as his *Guru*. He said, "I am still in search of one, and so far my feeling in regard to every one whom I might think of as a *Guru* has been 'No not this'. One must have requisite qualification to come under a perfect *Guru* and I cannot claim to have it."[15] Here lies the unseen catch. Gandhi never tried for his own salvation like *Rishis* or *Munis* wherein he needs a *Guru's* hand as a support to swim across the tribulations and sorrow inherent in society for safety leaving behind millions in this quagmire. He never practised his improvement in isolation. On the contrary he tried and endeavoured to improve society and the individual.

From the Sufi mystic Gandhi learnt to aspire a pure heart and love of God. In Sufi's love of God there is no hatred to any one, even to the devil. One hates devilish acts but not devil. This became the content and core of the Gandhian thought in politics and economics. He hated the acts of the opponent but not the opponent. He hated capitalism but not the capitalist. A Sufi sees the cross and the church, but does not see God on the cross or in the church. Similarly he neither finds God in a temple or a mosque nor in Herat or in Kandhar. Neither the cave nor the hill top becomes the abode of God.[16] He is found in the heart of man; the spring of love and compassion. Love and compassion kill the hatred. Hatred is momentary Love is eternal. Love triumphs. Ultimately love and compassion for the fellow beings become one of the main tenets of Gandhi's religion. At this stage his religion cuts across all religions and sticks to the inner core of all religions.

The same aspect he found in the Christianity with which his interaction was much when compared with other religions save Hinduism. Concept of "sinlessness" Gandhi saw in the life and teachings of Christ. "He had deep reverence for Jesus Christ. He saw Jesus Christ without the appendages of theology, dogma and doctrine. He believed that Christianity could become still better and purer, if

Theosophy'. This book made him to read books on Hinduism.[5] He realised what the missionaries preached about Hinduism was false.

Gandhi met good many Christians. Read the *Old Testament*. He read the book of Genesis. The 'Sermon on the Mount' went straight into his heart.[6] He read Carlyle's 'Heroes and Heroworship'. Prophets' bravery, greatness and austere living attracted him. All this stimulated him to read more books on religion. He read Mrs. Besant's, 'How I became a Theosophist". This revealed him how she was turned to theism from atheism. He read Charles Bradlaugh who was an atheist. Gandhi admired and respected him.

Gandhi being a *Sanatanist*, believed that the *Gita* formed the essence of the 'mighty *Vedas*' and the 'lofty *Upanishads*'.[7] He understood the importance of the relation between *Bhakti* and *Jnana*. The former accompanied by the latter leads to the service without the thoughts of reward.[8] He felt self realization is possible through *Gita*.[9] The principle of service to all people with equal regard envisioned in concluding words of Socrates at the time of his trial that nothing harms a goodman either in this world or the next and God never forsakes goodmen.[10] This produced requisite resonance in Gandhi.

Gandhi was much influenced by the writings of Shrimad Raichand. Gandhi always felt that Shrimad writings breathe the spirit of truth. He did not write a single word in order to show off his knowledge. His aim in his writings was to share his inward bliss with his readers.[11] Gandhi wrote "I am sure that any one who wishes to free himself with inner conflict and is eager to know his duty in life will gain much from Shrimad's writings, whether such a reader is a Hindu or belongs to another faith."[12]

In South Africa, Gandhi came into contact with some Christians. Their lives were pure. They were good men. They were devoted to religion. They tried to foist Christianity on Gandhi. Gandhi wrote, "Though I had come into contact with them in connection with practical affairs, they began to feel solicitude for my spiritual welfare. I realised that I had one duty; that until I had studied the teachings of Hinduism and found that they do not satisfy my soul, I should not renounce the faith in which I was born. I, therefore, started reading Hindu and other scriptures. I read books on Christianity and Islam. I carried on correspondence with some friends I had made in London. I placed doubts before them"[13]. With this scepticism he

was that divinity in man subdues evil in him paving the way for nonviolence and towards truth.

Keeping this aim of nonviolence and truth he looked at every religion with reverence. Every religion offered something or the other. The result was that the reality of nonviolence and its efficacy were clearer and clearer to him in his journey towards Truth. He could see the core of all religions. He could see "*Kripan* (of the Sikhs) as a symbol of sanctity to be exhibited and spent in defence of the helpless, and the innocent."[27] Similarly Gandhi had interpreted *Koran*. He found *Koran* was based on nonviolence not on violence.[28] Prophethood is attained by wrestling with God but not by wielding sword. The master key thus to understand the underlying unity of all religions is truth and nonviolence.[29]

Gandhi could not transcend beyond the conflict between reason and faith. "For a while he was practically an atheist. Upto a point he had worshipped the God honestly. He had never, since the age of reasoning, imagined that the stone or wood or metal image was itself a God, but he had been told and believed that an act of consecration endowed the image with a Divine spirit, and this localised spirit he worshipped. His companionship with other minds, however, almost imperceptibly changed his conception of religion. He became sceptical. A strong natural tendency to analytical study made him question the why at every thing".[30] And every aspect of religion he judged from the angle of nonviolence. He further interpreted accordingly. He could see the meaning of life in the writings of Socrates, Buddha, Solomon and Schopenhauer.

Gandhi could see some connection of his vision in the thinking of Tolstoy. He was more attracted to him. The latter's love of detachment from wealth and affluence as an instrument for peace in public relations and love in individual life,[31] opened vistas to Gandhi. To him it is one of the early steps to bring harmony in society and finally for the establishment of a nonviolent society.

What is the justification of violence? There are three premises for the existence of violence, but not its justification. People feel that violence is inherent in society and social relations. Firstly that coercion of man by man existed in all ages and will continue to exist. It is a fact. But the conscience of man pushes him to embrace love and compassion towards his fellow being. Gandhi searched this aspect strife and conflict. Conflict and strife can be removed by crucifying oneself. Life survived amidst death. Birth is an eternal event so is the cross. "A living Christ means a living cross. Without it life is a living death.[21] To mitigate the suffering one has to lead a life of true Christian. This became the corner stone of Gandhian ethics if not religion.

The gospel of love in Buddhism attracted Gandhi. In this regard he was more near to Buddhism than the other religions. He considered the Buddha as the greatest preacher of peace. He wrote: "I have the greatest veneration for the Buddha. He is one of the greatest preachers of peace. The gospel of the Buddha is the gospel of love."[22] Apart from the gospel of love he understood *Nirvana* in a different way. "*Nirvana* is undoubtedly not utter extinction. So far as I (Gandhi) was able to understand the central fact of Buddha's life *Nirvana* is utter extinction of all that is base in us. *Nirvana* is not like the black dead peace of the grave, but the living peace, the living happiness of a soul which is conscious of itself and conscious of having found its own abode in the heart of Eternal."[23] Buddhist contribution to humanity lies in its teaching to regard for all life. Sanctity of life whether human or animal was upheld by the Buddhist. This aspect in Buddhism attracted Gandhi much. Further the concept of prayer in Buddhism was understood by Gandhi in secular context. Prayer invoked divinity in man. Divinity raises man to higher levels and thus he gets purified. Buddhism is a long prayer to remove the baser instinct and improve man. Prayer guides man towards a moral government and moral society. Man is steered through selfishness. Buddhism in a way is synopsis of Gandhi's religious thought.

Gandhi interpreted scriptures of every religion in support of nonviolence. To him every scripture mirrors truth. The result was that whoever interpreted any religion or commented in terms of nonviolence was appreciated and had space in Gandhi's columns.[24] He in turn interpreted religious writings in terms of nonviolence. He searched truth and nonviolence in all the writings. He always supported any comments or analysis or reasoning of religious writings that had gone against violence.[25] While commenting on *Guru Granth Saheb* Gandhi wrote : "I hold *Granth Saheb* in high reverence.... it inculcates faith, valour and an invincible belief in the ultimate triumph of right and justice."[26] The entire theme of Gandhian idea of religion

To Gandhi religion means the principle enunciated in the Sermon on the Mount with the elucidation from the *Gita*. In the light of this Ishopanishad of the *Upanishads* has to be understood and practised in structuring the man, so that the principle of *Ahimsa* becomes the operative formula and makes the individual a true *Satyagrahi* not merely for political purposes but helps towards the movement of society. The three things which Gandhi valued in *Ishopanishad* are: 'Renounce it and enjoy it. Enjoy what He gives you. Do not covet any body's wealth or possession.'

"This *Mantra* has to be understood in the light of the teachings in the *Gita*. Similarly the *Gita* has to be understood in the light of this *Mantra* of *Ishopanishad*."[40] Further Gandhi felt that this *Mantra* satisfies the cravings of a socialist, a communist, a philosopher and an economist.[41] Again it also caters to the thinking of those who do not belong to Hindu fold.[42]

From this angle the word *Dharma* which the Gandhians associated with Gandhi's idea of religion is framed and identified with the word religion. The words religion and *Dharma* are viewed as similar to each other. The result was that Gandhi was interpreted in religious terms as understood in the common parlance. Taking an overview of the Gandhian ideals and his political aim one could see that the word *Dharma* leans not on religion as understood but on obligations—obligations towards fellowmen, towards one's own group, the state and society. If further analysed what this word *Dharma* meant is that it denotes the inbuilt input in Gandhian society to soften and to remove friction between social groups on one hand and on the other the individual and society. This ultimately culminates into the establishment of a frictionless society and gradually rooting out exploitation. The medium through which it is possible is to operate the principle of *Ahimsa*. The aim of frictionless society is *Sarvodaya*. This does not mean an evolutionary process. At every stage Gandhi was for revolution. He was a reformer vis-a-vis a freedom fighter. He was always in hurry. Only limitation was *Ahimsa*.

Gandhi's ideas on religion attracted the common masses as well as the Indian intellectuals, nurtured both in the Western and the Eastern institutions.

The common man was educated in certain aspects of Hinduism like *Varna Ashrama Dharma*, cow protection and *Brahmacharya*.

indulgence and multiplication of wants as these hamper one's growth to the ultimate identity with the universal self."[38]

From this high pedestal Gandhi tries to bring certain ideals of Hinduism on to the mundane plane and explained to the masses. With him the sole passion and purpose was to bring the masses on to the main stream of struggle for freedom and making them alive to the grim realities like communal discord, untouchability etc., present in the Indian society. In this direction the radicals of the radicals could not hold candle to him. Gandhi was on the left of left. He explained the demand of religion on man through his pet themes of cow protection, *Brahmacharya*, etc. By and large the intellectual failed to grasp the meaning of his pet themes. The masses followed him because he could talk to them in their language and idiom. On the other hand when Gandhi began to speak religious tolerance and unity in religion the intellectual tried to understand him. And mystics appreciated him when he elaborated his concept like divinity in man and ethics textured religion. Therefore, Gandhi appeared to Indian intellectual as conservative if not obstructionist altogether. Where the masses were involved fully the intellectual dare not call him so. They acquiesced in his plan of action but not in his thought. His political heir apparent Jawaharlal Nehru used to declare often that he was associated with Gandhi in action but not in thought.

Gandhi looked at religion as the fountain head of mercy and compassion. And religion is the basis of ethics to him and nothing else. Gandhi quoted Tulsidas : "The root of religion is embedded in mercy, where as egotism is rooted in the love of the body, Tulsi says that mercy should never be abandoned, though the body perishes."[39] From this is the importance of *Ahimsa* as an operational medium springs out.

Thus Gandhi picked secular ideas with high moral content and weaved these into a religious thought. This is the essence of religion in Gandhi. He never accepted any tenet that inhibits the growth of man. He favoured religion not theology to sow the seeds of ethics in man. This was one of the reasons he did not go whole hog for religious reform. His entire discourse on religion is to bring out the best in man. He attacked fanaticism. He also condemned these religious practices which go against *Ahimsa* like animal sacrifice. Beyond this, his roar against any other religious practice and creed remained unheard and subdued.

To Gandhi religion means the principle enunciated in the Sermon on the Mount with the elucidation from the *Gita*. In the light of this Ishopanishad of the *Upanishads* has to be understood and practised in structuring the man, so that the principle of *Ahimsa* becomes the operative formula and makes the individual a true *Satyagrahi* not merely for political purposes but helps towards the movement of society. The three things which Gandhi valued in *Ishopanishad* are: 'Renounce it and enjoy it. Enjoy what He gives you. Do not covet any body's wealth or possession.'

"This *Mantra* has to be understood in the light of the teachings in the *Gita*. Similarly the *Gita* has to be understood in the light of this *Mantra* of *Ishopanishad*."[40] Further Gandhi felt that this *Mantra* satisfies the cravings of a socialist, a communist, a philosopher and an economist.[41] Again it also caters to the thinking of those who do not belong to Hindu fold.[42]

From this angle the word *Dharma* which the Gandhians associated with Gandhi's idea of religion is framed and identified with the word religion. The words religion and *Dharma* are viewed as similar to each other. The result was that Gandhi was interpreted in religious terms as understood in the common parlance. Taking an overview of the Gandhian ideals and his political aim one could see that the word *Dharma* leans not on religion as understood but on obligations—obligations towards fellowmen, towards one's own group, the state and society. If further analysed what this word *Dharma* meant is that it denotes the inbuilt input in Gandhian society to soften and to remove friction between social groups on one hand and on the other the individual and society. This ultimately culminates into the establishment of a frictionless society and gradually rooting out exploitation. The medium through which it is possible is to operate the principle of *Ahimsa*. The aim of frictionless society is *Sarvodaya*. This does not mean an evolutionary process. At every stage Gandhi was for revolution. He was a reformer vis-a-vis a freedom fighter. He was always in hurry. Only limitation was *Ahimsa*.

Gandhi's ideas on religion attracted the common masses as well as the Indian intellectuals, nurtured both in the Western and the Eastern institutions.

The common man was educated in certain aspects of Hinduism like *Varna Ashrama Dharma*, cow protection and *Brahmacharya*.

indulgence and multiplication of wants as these hamper one's growth to the ultimate identity with the universal self."[38]

From this high pedestal Gandhi tries to bring certain ideals of Hinduism on to the mundane plane and explained to the masses. With him the sole passion and purpose was to bring the masses on to the main stream of struggle for freedom and making them alive to the grim realities like communal discord, untouchability etc., present in the Indian society. In this direction the radicals of the radicals could not hold candle to him. Gandhi was on the left of left. He explained the demand of religion on man through his pet themes of cow protection, *Brahmacharya*, etc. By and large the intellectual failed to grasp the meaning of his pet themes. The masses followed him because he could talk to them in their language and idiom. On the other hand when Gandhi began to speak religious tolerance and unity in religion the intellectual tried to understand him. And mystics appreciated him when he elaborated his concept like divinity in man and ethics textured religion. Therefore, Gandhi appeared to Indian intellectual as conservative if not obstructionist altogether. Where the masses were involved fully the intellectual dare not call him so. They acquiesced in his plan of action but not in his thought. His political heir apparent Jawaharlal Nehru used to declare often that he was associated with Gandhi in action but not in thought.

Gandhi looked at religion as the fountain head of mercy and compassion. And religion is the basis of ethics to him and nothing else. Gandhi quoted Tulsidas : "The root of religion is embedded in mercy, where as egotism is rooted in the love of the body, Tulsi says that mercy should never be abandoned, though the body perishes."[39] From this is the importance of *Ahimsa* as an operational medium springs out.

Thus Gandhi picked secular ideas with high moral content and weaved these into a religious thought. This is the essence of religion in Gandhi. He never accepted any tenet that inhibits the growth of man. He favoured religion not theology to sow the seeds of ethics in man. This was one of the reasons he did not go whole hog for religious reform. His entire discourse on religion is to bring out the best in man. He attacked fanaticism. He also condemned these religious practices which go against *Ahimsa* like animal sacrifice. Beyond this, his roar against any other religious practice and creed remained unheard and subdued.

inferiority is the result of ignorance and the urge of man to exploit his fellowmen for his selfish ends.

To explain further secular principles like duty and livelihood, he took the assistance of the *Gita* a purely religious book. He borrowed the idea of "equality of spirit"[45] from the *Gita*. And declared that spiritual equality is the basis for equality in all other spheres. The duty and livelihood of man do not determine either equality or inequality. Gandhi while discussing *Varna Ashrama Dharma* wrote : "In an age where competition is held to be the law of life, and the possession is the largest measure of the world's goods *summum bonum*, and when everyone counts oneself free to follow any calling one likes, this attempt to hold up *Varna* as the law of life may well be regarded as an ideal dream and an attempt to revive it as childish folly. Be that as it may, it is my firm conviction that it is true socialism. In the language of the *Gita*, it is equality of spirit, without which no other equality is possible. The performance of it, no matter how slight, bodes well both for him who performs it and for the rest of mankind.

"It may add that though the *Varnas* are four, the number is not in my opinion unalterable. In the future reconstruction the number may be even more or even less than four. What is essential is that one must seek one's livelihood and no more from following the vocation to which one is born."[46]

Thus from each and every institution Gandhi had taken the requisite principle to educate the ignorant as well as the intellectual about the requirement of the individual. His emphasis is more on the secular ideas inherent in these Hindu institutions. This was not to glorify religion. The aim was to give religious colour and flavour to catch the imagination of the ignorant and poor, whose involvement in revolution was essential to break the establishment of exploitation. In this connection agreeing with the view of Max Muller the great indologist, Gandhi wrote : "was it not Max Muller who said that it was Hinduism more than any other religion that life was no more no less than duty?"[47]

In Gandhi's scheme of things the next important item was cow protection. Cow is very dear to the Hindu heart. He sees his salvation in the protection of cow. It touches the bile and blood of any Hindu. In cow protection Gandhi saw more than mere cow protection. To him protection of the cow means protection of the weak, the meek, the helpless, the dumb and deaf. He wrote to Jawaharlal Nehru in one of his letters; "Cow protection to me is definitely more than mere protection of the Cow. The cow is merely a type for all that lives. Cow protection means protection of the weak, the helpless, the dumb and the deaf. Man becomes then not the lord master of all creation but he is a servant. The cow to me is a sermon on pity."[48]

If the discussion is stretched further Gandhi looked beyond a society to emerge after the proletariat and peasant victory over his exploiters, wherein human being frees himself from chains. But sub-human life remains exploited by the man for his selfish interest. His vision postulates this eventuality. The logical culmination of nonviolence to its final fulfilment remains unattained.

What exactly Gandhi dreamt and meant in cow protection? To him it is just a symbol in his relentless endeavour to educate the people in the unity of life. In any system the weak are always exploited. Entire political speculation is to devise method and a structure to remove exploitation. If for a moment one thinks establishment of a state where there will be no exploitation, man being an animal will definitely try to exploit the animal world thinking that this planet full of life belongs to him, but not to others where life dwells but devoid of intelligence. Gandhi had chosen appropriate symbols to explain his view and concept which are primarily of religious origin yet, rich in secular and ethical content. He saw God in the unity of life.

Elaborating his principle of *Ahimsa* in the context of cow protection Gandhi further pointed out that a Hindu is never selfish in protecting the cow. He never kills her when she ceases to give milk. It is not the case in other countries. In the protection of cow he had not seen any religious ritual nor religious significance but his own religious belief i.e. the unity of life and the importance of life on this planet. This principle of religion became clear when Gandhi declared that "I shall not hate even a traitor. My religion takes me to that length."[49] To him life is important. He wrote : "My nonviolence is not merely kindness to all living creatures. The emphasis is laid on the sacredness of subhuman life. But that can never mean that one is to be kind to this life in preference to human life. While writing about the sacredness of such life I take it that sacredness of human life had been taken for granted. The former has been over emphasised and, while putting into practice the idea has undergone distortion."[50]

Again in the observance of *Brahmacharya* Gandhi looked for yet a different idea. He found means in restructuring man. *Brahmachari* does not mean mere celibacy. In Gandhian lexicon it means securing control over body and mind to get victory in the end. It has nothing to do with sex. Of course control of sex or senses is very much there but forms a minor part of *Brahmacharya*. Whereas the root meaning of *Brahmacharya* says search for truth, *charya* means course of conduct adopted to the search of *Brahma*, i.e. truth. From this etymological meaning arises the special meaning viz. "control of senses."[51] Further elaborating Gandhi wrote, "The true *Brahmachari* will shun false restraints. He must create his own fences according to his limitations breaking them down when he feels that they are unnecessary. The first thing is to know what true *Brahmachari* is, then to realise its value and lastly to try to cultivate this priceless virtue. I hold that true service of the country demands this observance."[52]

Numerous precepts relating to religion on which he spoke can be taken out and secular meaning embedded can be picked up in these. He picked up those secular concepts which have direct bearing on restructuring man, but not on theology. His religion is ethical religion. At numerous places and innumerable times Gandhi had spoken the importance of reason and enlightenment. While selecting these ideas from religious lore he kept his aim always as a guiding principle besides reason and enlightenment. He knew that knowledge and compassion ultimately lead to salvation.

Gandhi's search for secular concepts and ethics in scriptures and religious writings continued till he disappeared from the Indian scene. Simultaneously he applied these ideas to purify the man. His study of scriptures of all the main religions convinced him to make ethics as the basis of human development. Skilfully he did not criticise religion. Its importance was evident to him from the point of view of morals and morality. As long as religion becomes the support of morals Gandhi never raised his finger against religion. But the moment religion departs from morality or morals he was restless. He was not for any religion. He was for the principle of unity and sacredness of life on this planet. In this direction if religion is important he did not hesitate for a moment to consider religion as an instrument in his battle to get succour to the weak and the poor.

At every stage, therefore, he tried to search truth in all religions. Though a rationalist he realised the importance of religion. This resulted into a persistent and uninterrupted search for truth in religious writings. This truth helps the growth of the individual and society.[53] It is common in all religions. Gandhi wrote : "I believe in the truth of all religions in the world. And since my youth upward it has been a humble but persistent effort on my part to understand the truth of all religions of the world and adopt and assimilate in my own thought, word and deed all that I have found to be best in those religions. The faith that I possess not only permits me to do so but renders its obligatory for me to take the best whatsoever source it may come."[54] To him "morals of a man was a matter of concern rather than a particular form of worship in a church, in a mosque or in a temple. The form of worship is an empty formula if it does not contribute to human growth."[55] At a later stage Gandhi said that "religion has its own contribution to man for human evolution."[56]

From this moral aspect Gandhi travelled towards equality of religions. The theory and logic was simple. To him, when ethics is the basis of religion, all forms of religion are equal. It is because the inner current of ethics is the same in all religions. Religon is valuable when its inner core becomes a super conductor to transmit moral growth in man and society. He vigorously appealed to the people to approach religious books of different religions with same reverence as the people of a particular faith read their own religious scriptures.[57] Hence he later declared that all prophets belong to humanity.[58]

In a subtle way keeping his aim before him, Gandhi asked those who feel that they have more of earthly and spiritual goods have to serve more to the community and remain more humble.[59] Here he was pointing at the Hindus conveying a political message. Hindus forming majority, he wanted them to serve others in the interest of the country. When a society becomes multireligious, social and lingual there is the possibility of sowing the seed of liberalism and nurturing liberalism. A plural society alone provides environment for the growth of liberalism. Before making this appeal to the majority community he wrote, "My Hinduism is not secretarian. It includes all that I know to be best in Islam, Christianity, Buddhism and Zoroastrianism. I approach politics as everything else in religious spirit. Truth is my religion and *ahimsa* is the only way of its realisation."[60] When Gandhi said 'my Hinduism' he was not referring Hinduism as such. He was referring to his concept of religion and his understanding of religion. He had always put before him certain fundamental rules and principles. These are eternal. He wrote "I have no difficulty in hitting upon the truth, because I go by certain fundamental maxims. Truth is superior to everything and I reject that conflict with it. Similarly that which is in conflict with nonviolence should be rejected. And on matters which can be reasoned out, that which conflict with reason must also be rejected."[61]

While preaching equality of religions Gandhi listed certain principles from various religions that had contributed towards the enrichment of spirituality on the Indian soil. *Ahimsa* was the greatest contribution of Hinduism to mankind. Similarly the belief in oneness of God and the truth of the brotherhood of man are the distinctive contribution to Indian National Culture. The spirit of service was the main gift of Christianity to India's culture. Christian missionary propaganda against us has woken up to certain abuses in our fold and thinking. In all this Gandhi's political message was clear and loud. He used religion as one of the potent instruments to improve the man and simultaneously he was instrumental to make the march on the road to struggle for freedom quicker. Those who failed to peep into this phenomenon considered Gandhi as conservative and orthodox often putting breaks to the political movement towards a radical ideology. People who saw this phenomenon at surface level considered Gandhi a man of God and religion. The entire gamut of Gandhian ideas on religion requires a thorough search and interpretation to draw impartial conclusions. Spirituality, political ideology and economic compulsions criss cross his religious ideas. Hence Gandhi appeared thoroughly inconsistent and contradictory. *Ahimsa* the operating principle towards *Sarvodaya* remained guiding star to Gandhi. He had to carry millions of this land to *sarvodaya* never sacrificing *Ahimsa*.

What was Gandhi's religion? or more specifically what was Gandhi's Hinduism? From the beginning Gandhi styled himself as a *Sanatana* Hindu. Why *Sanatana* Hindu? He gave reasons for calling himself a *Sanatana* Hindu. His reasons are four.[62] Firstly he believed in the *Vedas*, the *Upanishads* and the *Puranas*. At this stage Gandhi's emphasis was on the philosophic content in these scriptures. The philosophic content is entirely different from theological content. As discussed earlier the secular content was carefully and methodically sifted and presented to the people in theistic medium. The aim was to restructure man. He took the help of the *Gita*. He knew that "a true votary of the *Gita* does not know what disappointment is."[63] And this is possible because of the principle, the "matchless remedy is renunciation of fruits of action."[64] In these two aspects there is nothing spiritual.

Second reason for calling himself a *Sanatana* Hindu was his belief in *Varna Ashram Dharma*. The third reason was his belief in cow protection. In the former he saw a universal law of life; duty or in a broader way work that keeps the belly full. In the latter he saw the principle of unity of life and sacredness of life.

The last i.e. the fourth reason to label himself a *sanatana* Hindu is his belief in idol worship. He wrote: "I have said I do not believe idol worship . An idol does not exercise any feeling of veneration in me. But I think an idol worship is a part of human nature. We hanker after symbolism. Why should one be more composed in a church than elsewhere? Images are an aid to worship. No Hindu considered an image to be God. I do not consider idol worship a sin."[65] What is God? All these questions crop up. These require answers. In the Gandhian literature these questions were answered fully. What is required is a careful and delicate sifting of universal secular matter from theology. His "Hinduism is not an exclusive religion. In it there is room for worship of all the prophets of this world. It is not a missionary religion in the ordinary sense of the term. It has no doubt absorbed many tribes in its fold, but this absorption has been evolutionary yet imperceptible in character. Hinduism tells every one to worship God according to his own faith or *Dharma*, and so it lives at peace with all religions"[66].

Gandhi's reference to Krishna, *Ramanama* and the words like these have definite meaning. He was aiming at an ideal level of life. He therefore made differentiation between historic Krishna and ideal Krishna. This distinction peels out theistic overtones in Gandhi's utterances and declarations.

Gandhi's interpretation of the *Gita* was on the lines of philosophy. According to him: "The key to an understanding of *Gita*, and the gist of it is that life is given to us for service and not for enjoyment. We have therefore to impart a sacrificial character to our lives. Intellectual assent to this proposition is only the firm step, but such assent and conduct in terms of that assent are bound to rid our heart of its perils in course of time. But what is real service? In order to obtain right answer to this question, restraint of senses is essential as it gives us clearer vision of the God of truth. Service rendered with selfish motives ceases to be sacrifice. Hence the urgent need for detachment. When this is understood, all manner of controversies lose their meaning for us. . . . when detachment governs our actions, even the weapons raised in order to strike an enemy fall out of our hand. But mere pretence of detachment may come to us, perhaps this very first day, or be only after thousand years. We must not worry over the time this takes, for the effort carries within itself the seeds of success. We must however be on our guard and make sure that it is genuine effort, and that there is no self deception and this certainly is possible for us."[67]

The spirit of service and selflessness have to be viewed from the point of knowledge and wisdom. What is knowledge? Knowledge of purity in man, selfless service and control of senses. Knowledge of these can be acquired through a book or a teacher or through humanity or earnestness or service. "While wisdom is not book learning. In it there is no room for doubt. It begins with faith and ends in experiences. It enables man to see all beings in himself and to see himself in God so that everything to him to be actually informed by God."[68] In certain things reason does not take one much far. These things have to be accepted by faith. And at this stage faith "does not contradict reason but transcends it. Faith is a kind of sixth sense which works in cases which are without purview of reason."[69]

Keeping this format Gandhi preaches for the creation of better Hindus, better Christians and better Muslims not merely traditional Hindus, Christians and Muslims. He wanted a religion which transcends traditional religions and aims at unity of religion and religious tolerance. At this stage essence of secular and moralist ideas can sprout and later to be nurtured on the religion seeped Indian soil. With this definite aim, because of environmental constraints Gandhi adopted theistic medium to educate his masses in secular ideas. He was successful. This clouded the vision of the Gandhians who could not see the reality in the layers of religious declarations of Gandhi.

REFERENCES

1. Karan Singh : *In Defence of Religion*, Vision Books Private Ltd., New Delhi, 1978. Preface p. V.
2. Gora : *An Atheist with Gandhi* : Navajeevan Publishing House, Ahmedabad; 1951. K. Mashuriwala in Introduction p. 20.
3. *In Search of the Supreme*, Vol. II : Navajeevan Publishing House, Ahmedabad 1961; p. 142.
4. Gandhian Thought, July 1970 : An article, Thomas Kepler.
5. 'Acquaintance with Religions'. *The Story of My Experiments With Truth*, Chapter XX (Part I), Navajivan Publishing House 1926.
6. *Ibid.*
7. Raghavan Iyer *The Moral and Political Writings of Mahatma Gandhi*, Vol. I, (Ed.), Clarendon Press, Oxford 1986, p. 84.
8. *Ibid.*
9. *Ibid.*
10. *Op. cit.*, p. 100
11. *Op. cit.*, p. 142
12. *Ibid.*
13. *Op. cit.*, p. 144
14. *Ibid.*
15. *Op. cit.*, p. 155
16. Interview with Abel, *The Hindu*, 3 May, 1929.
17. K.L. Sheshagiri, *Mahatma Gandhi and C.F. Andrews : A study in Hindu-Christian dialogue* : Punjabi University, Patiala : 1969, p. 3.
18. *Young India*, 31 December, 1931.
19. *Ibid.*
20. *Ibid.*
21. *Ibid.*
22. *Harijan*, 28 August, 1938.
23. *Young India*, 24 November, 1927.
24. *Young India*, 1st September, 1927.
25. *Young India*, 29th April, 1926.
26. *Young India*, 19th March, 1931.
27. *Harijan*, 7th December, 1947.
28. *Harijan*, 13th July, 1940.
29. *Ibid.*
30. Joseph J. Doke, *M.K. Gandhi : An Indian Patriot in South Africa*. Publications Division, 1967, New Delhi, p. 29.

31. Kalidas Nag, *Tolstoy and Gandhi*, Pustak Bhandar, Patna, 1950, p. 17.
32. *In Search of the Supreme*, Vol. III, p. 114.
33. *Op. cit.*, p. 89.
34. *Ibid.*, p. 89.
35. *Op. cit.*, p. 88.
36. *Young India,* 8 April, 1928.
37. *Harijan,* 8 December, 1947.
38. *Harijan,* 8 December, 1936.
39. *Harijan,* 30 November, 1947.
40. *Harijan,* 30 January, 1937.
41. *Ibid.*
42. *Ibid.*
43. M.K. Gandhi, *Hind Swaraj*, Navajeevan Publishing House, Ahmedabad 1984, p. 92.
44. *Harijan,* 28 September, 1934.
45. *Ibid.*
46. *Ibid.*
47. *Young India,* 17 November, 1927.
48. *Jawaharlal Nehru* : Bunch of Old Letters, p. 42.
49. *Young India,* 1 January, 1925.
50. *Harijan*, 9 January, 1946.
51. M.K. Gandhi : *From Yerwada Mandi* : Translated in English by V.G. Desai, Chapter III, 1957.
52. *Harijan,* 15 June, 1947.
53. *Harijan,* 30 January, 1937.
54. *Harijan,* 16 January, 1934.
55. *Harijan*, 30 January, 1937.
56. *Harijan*, 28 January, 1939.
57. *Harijan*, 13 March, 1937.
58. *Harijan*, 26 June, 1947.
59. *Harijan*, 25 March, 1937.
60. *Harijan*, 30 April, 1938.
61. *Harijan*, 6 March, 1937.
62. *Young India,* 6 October, 1921.
63. *Harijan*, 24 August, 1934.
64. *Young India*, 6 August, 1931.
65. *Young India*, 6 October, 1921.
66. *Young India*, 6 October, 1921.
67. M.K. Gandhi. *In Search of the Supreme,* Vol. III, Navajivan Publishing House, Ahmedabad, 1962, p. 239.
68. M.K. Gandhi. *In Search of the Supreme*, Vol. III, Navajivan Publishing House, Ahmedabad, p. 241.
69. *Op. cit.*, p. 18.

3

Gandhi and God, Prayer, Faith and All That

GOD, prayer, faith and other words of this kind were used to convey a definite meaning like the word religion employed by Gandhi to comprehend social phenomenon and to devise means to bring out a desired change in society and man. All these words have therefore definite and distinct meaning wherever Gandhi had used these. But these words are utilized in such a way that the theistic content and colour dominate more than the secular meaning and the secular utility. It is, therefore, necessary to peel off this thick coat over these words to know the secular content embodied therein. And then only, the method employed and the aim of Gandhi will be clear.

What is God? A hackneyed question. Any answer is hackneyed. Gandhi used very often words like God and religion. His critics and friends called this phenomenon as "God stunt".[1] He did not use this word much. But his readers and those who were bewildered by his personality asked numerous questions at numerous times. The result was that he had to perforce explain the meaning of these theological concepts to convey secular ideas retaining the theological mask. Hence wrong signals emanated. Even the grip of theology became strong and powerful. Gandhi could have conveyed his secular concept freely. But constraints of theology hindered him. The theological veil consciously employed by him to achieve a definite purpose could not be uncovered. The lesser mortals could not see the rationalist streak in Gandhian writings. They joined the bandwagon of people stamping Gandhi as a saint, even though Gandhi himself denied sainthood.

Gandhi could see some mysterious power in the movement of this universe and the life and death phenomenon in the human, animal and plant world. He felt this power.[2] He believed that this power is the centre of nature. It governs the life according to its plan. Life will be easier if it moves according to divine plan. It is only the interference of lesser mortals brings evil and calamity. Gandhi advised us to have faith in the benevolence of nature. He wrote: "This indefinable mysterious power pervades everything. I feel it though I do not see it. It is this unseen power which makes itself felt and yet defies all proof, because it is so unlike all that I perceive through my senses. It transcends the senses."[3] This mysterious force was termed as God. To reason out the existence of God is not possible. Or at the most in a limited way it can be reasoned. There is some method and rhythm in the result of some "unalterable law".[4] Even the matter has life. The life momentum explains the "orderliness in the Universe".[5] According to Gandhi : "That all then which governs all life is God. Law and the law giver are one. I may not deny the law or law giver, because I know so little about it or Him. Even as any denial or ignorance of the existence of an earthly power will avail me nothing, nor will my denial of God and His law liberates me from its operation; whereas humble and mute acceptance of divine authority makes life's journey easier even as the acceptance of earthly rule under it easier."[6]

At this stage, that is at the stage of recognising the 'mysterious power' the trend of nature, Gandhi did not identify this force as God. He was just accepting the facts both earthly and non-earthly which he conceived with senses or otherwise. He was still searching for the divine authority. The next stage was the answer to the question: What is divine authority ? In his discourses on the *Gita* at one stage Gandhi wrote : "Among the signs of the divine are fearlessness, purity of heart, wisdom, evenness of temper, self control, alms giving, sacrifice, study of scriptures, austerity, straight forwardness, nonviolence, truth, freedom from anger, renunciation, peacefulness, not speaking ill of others, compassion to all living beings, absence of greed, quietness, modesty, absence of fickleness, vigour, forgiveness, fortitude, purity, internal as well as external, freedom from malice and pride."[7] In short the qualities that are essential for the growth of the man in his elevation towards selflessness and action are divine qualities. These qualities which lift the man from the darkness of selfishness, he asserts in the operation of divine law and tries to recognise the importance of life in this universe.

One has to know whether this power is benevolent or malevolent. To Gandhi it was purely benevolent and soul satisfying power. His argument was that amidst death and destruction, life and creativity persist. In the midst of untruth, truth prevails. In the midst of darkness light shines. Therefore, Gandhi could see divine creativity, truth and light in life.[8] All these concepts are secular and nonreligious in character and content. In this context theology does not penetrate into this line of argument and thought.

After identifying divine qualities, Gandhi declared that these qualities are located in man the highest form of life on the earth. He placed importance to action and selfless service. Thus to him the meaning of God is the "sum total of *Karma*" that which impels the man to do right is God.[9]

While commenting on God from the political pulpit and writing in his *Young India*, Gandhi floated on the higher realm of Indian philosophy. At the outset he compared his concept of God with love. He identified God with love and compassion. And later jumped into another idea where he found that God is identical with truth. And finally to him truth is God. He vacillated between these two ideas : God is love and God is truth.[10] He wrote, "I then found that the nearest approach to truth was through love. But I also found that love has many meanings in the English language, at least human love in the sense of passion could become a degrading thing also. I found too, that love in the sense of *Ahimsa* had a limited number of votaries in the world. I never found a double meaning in connection with truth and not even atheist had demurred to the necessity or power of truth. But in their passion for discovering truth atheists have not hesitated to deny the very existence of God from their own point of right. And it was because of this reasoning that I saw that rather than say that God is truth I should say that Truth is God."[11]

From love Gandhi migrated to truth to identify God. Love and truth are divine qualities in man. In other words man can improve or improves with these divine qualities. Love is more or less an outer manifestation. It is visible. While truth is inner manifestation in man. not visible yet powerful to propel man towards further refinement.

The journey from 'God is Truth' to 'Truth is God' indicates the relative importance of God and Truth. Gandhi wrote: "I have come to the conclusion that for myself God is Truth. But two years ago I went a step further and said that Truth is God. You will see the fine distinctions between these two statements viz. that God is Truth and Truth is God. And I came to that conclusion after a continuous and relentless search after Truth which began nearly fifty years ago."[12]

In all religions the prophet and the scripture emphatically declare that God alone exists and the rest does not. To get a clear conception one has to look from a reverse direction. In other words that which does not exist is not truth. It means truth does not change with the time. It was same in the past. It remains same in the present and it will remain same in future. This is the simplest meaning any one can conceive and visualise.

Next important question in this discovery is : What is the meaning of truth in Gandhian terms. His answer in his own words. "A difficult question, but I have solved it for myself by saying that it is what the voice within tells you."[13] This inner voice according to Gandhi was conscience. Thus Gandhi used a powerful secular concept and presented to the world rather to the masses on whom he relied for his fight against colonialism, injustice and violence in theological terms. In a broader sense the divine qualities in man have to be roused to strengthen him for his betterment. With this recognition of divine qualities in man, Gandhi diverted the human dynamo in the service of man. Thus the divine qualities in man will blossom. Thus Gandhi saw God face to face in the service of man removing suffering. "Seeing God means realisation of the fact that God abides in one's heart"[13] To elucidate this point, in some other context he wrote: "I claim to know my millions. All the twenty-four hours of the day I am with them. They are my first care and the love, because I recognise no God except the God that is to be found in the heart of the dumb millions. They do not recognise his presence, I do and I worship the God that is truth or truth which is God through the service of the millions"[14] In a different context Gandhi again said : "We may not know God, but we know his creation. Service of his creation is the service of God."[15] Thus truth and service to humanity converge in Gandhian theology. In other words, his theology is secular concepts in theistic language intelligible and palatable to religion drunk masses on religion seeped soil.

After educating the importance of selfless service, Gandhi embarked on a plan to make oneself fit to get involved into selfless service. It is more appropriate to call this plan as a technique. To make it more appealing Gandhi called this as a technique to realise God. His definition and explanation of God remains the same viz. realisation of truth is possible only when one is involved in the selfless service towards others. *Brahmacharya* is one of the means towards this end. God is the force and essence of life. Man being the highest form of life can realise God through *Brahmacharya.* Devotees and sages like Tulsidas have shown the way. In a very mystical way Gandhi told that revitalisation of oneself is possible through *Brahmacharya.* To him in this regard it is essential. Gandhi wrote much on this aspect. *Brahmacharya*: *Brahmacharya* like other concepts *Varna Ashrama Dharma*, and cow protection has to be viewed in a different way. The subtle meaning attached to *Brahmacharya* had to be isolated and co-ordinated with the concept 'God realisation' as visualised in Gandhian vision. *Brahmacharya* has both narrow and wider meaning.[17] The accepted meaning of *Brahmacharya* is the attainment by man complete control over the sex organ.[18] It refers to the ordinary accepted sense of *Brahmacharya.* It means control in thought, word and action of animal passion.[19] And it is quite proper thus to restrict its meaning.

In the wider sense *Brahmacharya* means bringing a healthy soul into a healthy body.[20] "When the body controls all the senses, it becomes healthy. It controls thought both in the waking state and sleeping state. Only then a healthy soul takes into abode. The soul grows healthy. This does not mean that a healthy body should necessarily be strong in flesh and bone. A brave soul often inhabits a lean body. After a certain stage the flesh diminishes in proportion to the growth of the soul. A perfectly healthy body may be very fleshless, as muscular body is often heir to many an ill. Even if it is apparently free from disease it is not immune from infection, contagious diseases and the like. A perfect body on the contrary is proof against all these. Incorruptible blood has the inherent virtue of resisting all infection."[21] Thus in wider-sense Gandhi looked at the concept of *Brahmacharya.* His aim was to make the body an abode of a pure and highest form of soul. This will lead to the taming of flesh leading to extinction of desire. At this stage man's endeavour becomes selfless and purposeful.

Realisation of truth requires selflessness. And selflessness follows when self gratification is denied. Nonviolence signifies and aims at universal love. It is possible only when self gratification is denied to make the way for selflessness. An average house holder cannot rise to the height of universal love. He cannot look upon all mankind as his own kith and kin. He creates fences around him. His love is limited. It is limited in space and intensity. The route therefore to truth is *Brahmacharya* via *Ahimsa*.

From this high pedestal *Brahmacharya* has to be viewed. Only then Gandhi's conception of it will be clear. "*Brahmacharya* is the first and firm step towards God realisation. The other physical benefits are secondary in nature."[22] In the pursuit of the physical gratification the main aim of *Brahmacharya* is lost. Full development of body and soul does not take place. This results into many a disease. Practice and technique of practising *Brahmacharya* is not the scope of this volume.

The root meaning of *Brahmacharya* brings out a different meaning altogether. '*Charya*' means course of conduct. *Brahma* means truth. "*Brahmacharya* is the conduct adopted in search of *Brahmah* i.e. Truth. From this etymological meaning arises special meaning viz. control of all senses. Incomplete definition of *Brahmacharya* restricts itself to the sexual aspect."[23] The result was confusion over the purpose of *Brahmacharya*. In its completeness to a perfect *Brahmachari*, Gandhi wrote : "Woman for a *Brahmachari* is not the 'door keeper' of Hell but is an incarnation of our Mother who is in Heaven."[24] To prove his point Gandhi finally quoted the *Gita*. He wrote: We are told in *Bhagvad Gita* (11:59) that when a man starves his senses, the object of those senses disappear from him, but not the yearning for them, the yearning too departs when he beholds the supreme, that is to say the truth or *Brahma*."[25]

God realisation is possible only when one controls his senses and thereby yearning which makes his action spring from selflessness. Selflessness brings man nearer to the supreme. In this context God and Supreme have to be understood from the Gandhian angle. Besides *Brahmacharya* on this trail prayer is a potential element to be leaned on. It is equally necessary to wade through the distinct meaning that Gandhi had given to the word prayer.

The entire conflict is not between the weak and the strong resulting in the exploitation of the former. This particular aspect was the main aim as well as the sole aim in Gandhian philosophy. To remain constantly on the road towards this end: selflessness and later God realisation Gandhi took the aid of certain things. These encompass religion and politics. In a very subtle way, yet forcefully pointed out the fact of eternal duel between good and evil in man. He wrote: "Man's destined purpose is to conquer old habits to overcome the evil in him and restore good to its right place. If religion does not teach us how to achieve this conquest it teaches us nothing."[26] To Gandhi for establishing a just society he felt that the conflict is between the good and evil. One has to strive for subduing the evil. The conflict between the weak and the strong resulting in the exploitation of the former will disappear with the triumph of good over evil in an exploiter. Gandhi thus always looked at religion to soften the fang, the claw and the sting in man. He viewed religion as a corpus of religious and secular ideas with emphasis on the unity of life. All this is possible if the individual is restructured to subdue evil in him. Coupling this with the Gandhian meaning of God i.e. Truth, and truth is the sanctity of life on this universe, prayer comes only when there is faith in the sanctity of life and unity of life. With the recognition of the sacredness of life in plant, animal and human the recognition of good in man takes place. The good in man propels him because of his divinity to move forward. In all religions this conflict has been painted as the duel between God and Satan in Islam and Christianity, and duel between Ahurmazd and Ahsiman in Zoroastrianism. "Prayer is an impossibility without a living faith in the presence of God within."[27] Prayer leads the individual to conquer evil within him. And when divinity vanquishes evil a true man is born. The establishment of a just society becomes automatic. Thus one has the capability to subdue evil in him.

Prayer should come from the inner depth of heart. "A heart felt prayer is not a recitation with the lips. It is an yearning from within which expresses itself in every word, every act, nay, every thought of man."[28] Gandhi called "prayer an absolute shield and protection against the trinity of evils."[29] : act, word and thought.

Prayer presupposes, "unlimitable patience"[30] and 'confession'.[31] Patience aims at control of the trinity of evil. It is practice which requires entire effort. Whereas confession aims at achieving sinlessness, sin can be wiped out by confession. "No mortal is a proof against error. Danger consists in concealing one's error, in aiding untruth in order to gloss it over."[32] These two aids reduce man to nothingness. Only then he is capable of prayer to purify himself.

To aim at a distinct meaning to prayer Gandhi made distinction between prayer and worship. "Prayer means asking God for something in a reverent attitude."[33] "Worshipping God means singing the praise of God. Prayer is a confession of one's unworthiness and weakness."[34] Prayer specially ignites the divinity in man. Confession of weakness and asking forgiveness to be better and to do better involves prayer. Prayer to some brings the desired result earlier and to some later. This depends upon the content quantum of divinity in man. The more man is divine the earlier he produces the inner strengths and cleanses the inner guilt.

Worship has a peculiar place in man's life. As it is the praising of the lord, it makes one to look into the qualities of God which are generally found in scriptures of all religions. The more one gets drawn to these morals and ethics, the more he is divine. Thus these qualities invoke moral qualities in man. He is not drawn to the evil in him. The importance of man turning from evil lies in prayer and worship. As these two have a definite place in refining man, prayer and worship are to be performed with heart not with lips.[35] This cleanses the heart. In other words divinity gets ignited and evil gets burnt. The restructuring of man takes place. God, prayer and worship merge into one to bring the desired change in the individual and then in society. In this phenomenon there is no religion as understood ordinarily. Therefore at a particular context Gandhi said: "That the prayer is the very soul and essence of religion, ethical religion and therefore prayer must be the very core of the life of man, for no man can live without religion."[36] Thus prayer and religion are necessary to inject ethical inputs in man. Thus the traditional meaning and importance of prayer do not touch Gandhi at all.

Further elaborating, Gandhi pointed out the prayer is of two types. one is petitional and the other an inward communion.[37] In both these cases the aim is to cleanse the heart. It is an attempt to get strength to dominate evil. Inbuilt restraints in man develop strength to subdue evil in him. Liberty gifted to man can easily be utilised to remove self indulgence. This is possible through prayer. Ethical fibre in man gets strengthened. At certain stages Gandhi did not elaborate rejuvenating effect in man to face his environment and sometimes hostile climate. The 'ungovernable brute' in man has to be kept under control. The entire attempt is self-purification and separation of man from his brutish ancestry. *Bhajans, Slokas, Mantras* and scriptures of every religion act to this effect. Prayer is addressed to ourselves not to God. It is to shake off our torpor.

To invoke divinity in man prayer helps and thus unites him with his Maker. Once this is recognised we reach near to truth. This truth is not merely expected to speak. It is that alone constitutes the stuff of which all things are made, "which subsists by virtue of its own power, which is not supported by anything else but supports which exists. Truth alone is eternal. Everything else is momentary."[38] This truth is the mysterious energy behind the momentum of this universe. Prayer is to stir the divinity in man to contribute his divine mite to the momentum of the universe. Prayer is for spiritual nutrition. It is a spiritual nutrient.

At a superficial level Gandhi appears as a votary of Hinduism in which he was born. But his religion is "Hinduism of his own"[39] The word *Ramanama* should not be identified with any Hindu connotation. It has to be understood in the meaning it enjoined in Gandhian lexicon. Familiarity and faith give strength to a word. For a Hindu specially for a *Vaishnav*, *Ramanama* is familiar word and evokes faith. Beyond that it has no special significance. The religious aspect of a Hindu is stirred by the word *Ramanama*. Similar is the case with certain words in other religions. These key words in religion like *Ramanama* in Hindu fold when uttered with a purpose even like a parrot go long way to help the man.[40] Thus one does not need any symbol. Because "the name of Rama is more powerful than Rama himself and suggests no relation between the word Rama and its meaning."[41] Repetition of the word should not be for show or deceit but to achieve the purpose for which one utters. The faith and familiarity would work like laser beam and give inbuilt strength.

Gandhi went further to separate Rama and Krishna from the historic sense. Both these great heroes have to be viewed as ideal persons symbolising man fully inspired by divinity within, but not as historic persons. History, imagination and truth have got so inextricably mixed up that it is next to impossible to disentangle them.[42] Rama is embodiment of truth wrapped in divinity. Divinity in man has to be restored. To this end repetition of *Ramanama* at heart helps. It helps those who want to strengthen the moral fibre within and who want to restrain themselves and cannot inspire of themselves.[43]

Besides self purification Gandhi wrote that *Ramanama* is useful for national service, and it can be used as a medicine for man for natural cure. It is a medicine for masses. *Ramanama* can be used for good. It is a sort of turning inward eye to see oneself. It is not for an evil purpose. Because conscience pricks. Heart does not accept. Divinity is a part of heart. Hence the latter accepts the former. Devilry is alien to heart. The latter pushes the former.

Thus at every stage in every context religion and symbols associated with it had been interpreted broadly and used to draw the best in man and thus to restructure him. In the course of explanation contradictions and inconsistencies do appear. But they are ironed out with a measuring rod of ethics. In Gandhian religion the purpose, the aim and the destination are clear. The ethical frame which is delicate and fragile in man has to be steeled. And divinity in him has to be roused.

Faith in divine qualities in man made Gandhi hope to improve man. This faith was nothing to do with faith as normally understood. The man who has faith in himself and the case for which he is pursuing never fails. This faith brings forth divinity in man. This gives strength. Hence Gandhi's advice was to seek first the Kingdom of Heaven within and other things will follow.[44] This *Mantra* of Gandhi leads to self purification and self sacrifice in man. To this end faith as understood is directed. This will make man to wield a weapon against violence the negative force in man. Gandhi wrote: "So long as we believe that all is from God we should have no cause for perturbation. The only condition is that whatever we do we should do with God as witness. It is he who makes the world go and we only reap consequences of our action."[45] At the outset it appears that these words are seeped in religion and God. But when these words are translated into Gandhian ideology it means the sanctity of life has to be preserved. It can be preserved through nonviolence alone. In the sanctity of life divine qualities are preserved and nurtured to improve man who symbolises the supreme form of life, where evil can be subdued by good leading into the kingdom of God within. And everything moves as per the plan of God, i.e. natural laws drive towards truth. Here Gandhi asked his followers to employ intellect, reason, and ability to foresee. But when all these fail he advised to place faith in the goodness of man.

Again, yet in a different context Gandhi wrote: "Remember that we have in this world no enemy greater than ourselves. The *Bhagavad Gita* proclaims it in almost every verse. If I was to sum up the teaching of the Sermon of the Mount I find the same answer. My reading of the *Koran* has led me to the same conclusion. No one can harm us so much as we can ourselves."[46] Repeatedly Gandhi told his followers to look inwardly to bring forth divine qualities and control evil within to march in step with laws of nature to reach Truth. He puts faith in divinity in man. The divinity in man makes him strong.

To make a *Satyagrahi* strong Gandhi told *Satyagrahis* to have faith in themselves and faith in divinity. He had clothed a religious raiment to this aspect for different reasons. He needed the support of the masses. When the masses follow him he had to explain this in the language the masses understood. Moreover he was leading the masses to fight against colonialism, exploitation and violence. He was clear in his aim. His purpose and destination were a part of final aim. Inputs in man have to be improved to bring out good in man. His faith is faith in man, but not faith in any religious creed.

Because of this unfailing faith in man, at every stage of failure Gandhi thought that these failures strengthen the man.[47] "Cleanses him from impurities."[48] Tribulation, trial and privation make the individual stronger and richer in experience. On the contrary happiness and comfort bring monotony and boredom. These do not propel him to move forward. *Ramayana* is a record of trials, privation and penance.[49] Similarly *Mahabharata* reminds that all human effort is fruitless and all human life ends in frustration. And in the agony of each character the agony of the world is experienced.[50]

At a different context in similar vein Gandhi explained the importance of faith in divinity in man. He wrote: "For a man of truth must ever be confident if he has also equal need to be different. His devotion to truth demands the fullest confidence. His consciousness of fallibility of human nature must make him humble and therefore ever ready to retrace his steps, immediately he discovers his error. It makes no difference to his confidence that he has previously made Himalayan blunders. His confession and penance make him, if anything, stronger for future action. Discovery of errors makes the votary of truth more cautious of believing things and forming conclusions, but once he has made up his mind, his confidence must remain unshaken. His errors may result in man's reliance upon his judgement being shaken, but he must not doubt the truth of his position once he has come to a conclusion. It should further be borne in mind that my errors have been errors of calculation and judging man, not in appreciating the true nature of truth and *Ahimsa* or in their application. Indeed these errors and my prompt confessions have made me surer, if possible, of my insight into the implications of the truth and *Ahimsa*. For I am convinced that my action in suspending civil disobedience at Ahmedabad, Bombay and Bardoli has advanced the cause of India's freedom and world peace. I am convinced that because of the suspensions we are nearer *Swaraj* than we would have without, and this I say in spite of despair being written in thick black letters on the horizon."[51] Gandhi suspended his movements whenever they had turned violent, deviated from the path of nonviolence. At the same time his faith in his method remained unshaken. It is because he wanted to strengthen the moral fibre in his *Satyagrahis*. Acceptance of deviation from the path of nonviolence means defect and disaster. He had tremendous faith in man's positive qualities, which he termed divinity in man. Even an iota of deviation from the path of nonviolence leads to suffering and succumbing to evil.

Asceticism like every other religious concept has a separate meaning in Gandhian thought. It aims at reducing wants. Turns the individual from materialistic view. Inculcates simple living and high thinking. It is key to happiness as it produces contentment. Individual at no stage becomes a slave to his desires. "As the sages have described from the house tops that man can be his worst enemy as well as his best friend. To be free or to be slave lies in his hands. What is true for the individual is true for society."[52] Thus Gandhi brought the principle of asceticism out from religious monasteries and *Ashramas* and applied to bring harmony in society rather than individual salvation. In all his declarations and discussions on religion individual salvation occupied no place. He wanted to purify the individual to remove friction in society.

An ascetic is one who cares for others and not for himself. To him the aim is to achieve self purification and selflessness and thus becoming an effective instrument in the improvement of society. Renunciation is the key in the hands of ascetic. He does not want anything which stimulates the instinct of possession. He is a well wisher and an excellent member of society. Penance and asceticism liberate the man from bondage to material things and comforts. According to Gandhi, an individual should attain *Swaraj* for himself first. Then he would be fit person to work for the *Swaraj* of others. In other words it produces requisite detachment that makes his work easier.

When an individual achieves a modicum of detachment, riches mean nothing to him. He of his own gradually embraces poverty. A society where men voluntarily move towards poverty or nonpossession is not inimical to other societies. To this end Gandhi wanted mortification of flesh. When the flesh is fully controlled and directed towards service of others mortification of flesh is not necessary.[53] In this case it is torture without any purpose and aim.

The aim behind penance, asceticism fasting, practices of periodic spells of silence is to remove evil in man. Any amount of preaching and explanation about the benefit of removing evil in man will not be effective. Religious raiment and coating to these are essential to make masses feel the potent effect of these. Hence Gandhi effected an effective medium which resembles theistic, yet secular and liberal in content, tone and texture.

In essence what is penance? And what is its technique? Penance aims at removing the internal mechanism which strengthens selfishness in man and thus make him invalid as an instrument of service to his fellow men. Selfishness is not at all necessary for self preservation. On the contrary selfishness inducts effluents into man and makes him redundant in society. He will become cancerous and the long term interests of society are sacrificed. When penance removes these germs of disease in man the quality of selflessness emerges. This leads to self realisation.

While explaining the technique of penance, Gandhi pointed out the relation between a wrong doer and penitent.[54] The former should have love for the latter. Only then penance for wrong doing and reformation of wrong doer do take place. Penance for the failure of others who do not respect penance will not solve any problems. Penance goes in vain. Only as *Mahatma*, a great soul takes penance for the sins of the whole world. Further one has to do penance if he is a party to wrong doing. Then only a wrong doer is corrected. Suffering gives licence to do penance. Again a penitent should be free from guilt and misconduct similar to wrong doer. Otherwise the desired effect will not be there. Penance becomes mockery. Penitent must have a person at interest to improve the group in which he lives. He should be free from anger. Penance should be the outcome of love. Because the objective is purification of oneself from guilt. Guilty should feel that he is getting purified or on the way of purification while undergoing penance. Penance should be undertaken against a wrong accepted by all and at the same time it is spiritually harmful. Penitent must be aware of this. The wrong done must be accepted by society as harmful. Then only penance attracts a wrong doer to repent at the sin he committed. This automatically brings out good in man, whereas punishment has negative effect and limited value to bring order in society. Thus in penance Gandhi had not seen any religion or theology. In the Gandhian scheme of things penance is one of the inputs to draw the best out of men.

Through these concepts Gandhi had directly touched certain rules and regulations essential for an Ashramite more so who are working with a mission to improve his fellow men. These are essential to men who have to be seeped into ethics. Some of the qualities Gandhi had emphasized were: fearlessness, bread, labour, non-stealing and non-possession, humility, control of palate etc.

Before going into these that are semireligious a quick look at *Ashram* rules and regulations will give an idea of Gandhi's attempt to inculcate discipline in his mission. They are:[55]

1. Utilise every minute of their to good account.
2. They will participate in corporate activity of the *Ashram*.
3. When free they will spin.
4. They will prosecute their private studies.
5. Idle talk and talk in loud voice are prohibited.

6. Relation between Ashramites should remain peaceful and truthful.
7. Guests should be looked after properly and affectionately.
8. Water should not be wasted.
9. Food must be taken like medicine under proper restraint to sustain body and to keep fit for service.
10. Food should be taken slowly, decorously and neatly.
11. Every one should wash their own plates.
12. Everything should be kept at its own place.

All these are some of the rules codified for observance. Some more rules were there. All these were to regulate the life of an Ashramite to make an effective soldier in the struggle for freedom. These rules and regulations hardly touch any religion or theology.

In knowing God what Gandhi called Truth, fearlessness is one of the qualities that follows prayer and meditation. What did Gandhi meant fearlessness to be? And how to cultivate fearlessness? In the answers to those questions divinity or spiritual concept do not appear nor visible. But a relentless drive to improve quality of human material is ever present. To Gandhi fearlessness was one of the divine attributes of man. He supported his argument taking one from the sixteenth Chapter in the *Gita*, wherein fearlessness is one of the qualities is enumerated. Fearlessness "implies freedom from delusion".[56] It is achieved by cultivating self confidence.[57]

To what constitutes fearlessness Gandhi wrote: "Fearlessness connotes freedom from all external fears---fear of disease, bodily injury and death, of dispossession of losing one's nearest and dearest, of losing reputation, or giving offence and so on. One who overcomes the fear of death does not surmount all other fears, as is commonly but erroneously supposed. Some of us do not fear death, but fear from the minor ills of life. Some are ready to die themselves, but cannot bear the loved ones being taken away from them. Some misers will put up with all this, will part even their lives, but not their property, others will do any number of black deeds in order to uphold their supposed prestige. Some will swerve from the straight and narrow path, which lies clear before them, simply because they are afraid of incurring the world's odium. The seeker of truth must conquer all these fears. He should be ready to sacrifice his all in the quest of truth, even as Harischandra did. The story of Harischandra may be only a parable, but every seeker will bear witness to its truth from his principle experience, and therefore that story is as precious as historical fact."[58] Fearlessness should instil courage to follow one's duties and principles. This would effect improvement in the quality of life.

The second question is how to cultivate fearlessness? The answer to this constitutes the crux of entire thing. Fear has two aspects both external and internal.[59] As stated earlier any calamity real or imaginary falls under the category of external fears. To remove external fears one has to be free from delusions. Internal fears constitute external fears. These are animal passion, anger and the like which make man to be guided by emotion and instinct but not by reason and enlightenment. Once these are kept under control if not conquered altogether the internal fear ceases, because it is the "baseless fabric of our own vision".[60] Fear automatically disappears the moment attachment to body is removed. There is inverse relation between these two. The more is the attachment the more is the fear. Once attachment to wealth, family, and body is removed fearlessness descends gracefully upon man, because nothing on earth belongs to him. Everything belongs to that unseen power which governs this earth with certain rules. There is a saying in the *Upanishads*: "To give up attachment while we enjoy them". That is to say enjoy as trustees but not as proprietors. The goal is to serve others as servants but not as masters. Thus fearlessness makes man an ideal instrument strong and sharp to be employed in the service of humanity. A fearless individual becomes a carrier to transport society to the higher stages, where exploitation becomes less and less giving recognition to the sanctity of life on this earth. It is truth to Gandhi. He gave this concept to masses wrapping with the word God Almighty. And Truth is always Almighty.

This entire principle of fearlessness and fear when brought on to the frame of revolution, revelations in polities will be more illuminating. This Gandhi clarified by saying that a terrorist is afraid of his victim hence kills him.[61] A fearless revolutionary fights violence through nonviolence. He is not afraid of his opponent and his exploiter. He approaches him with the creed of nonviolence but not with the stick of violence.

Greed is different kind of fear. It makes man animal. Because of attachment he feels frightened. He thinks that he cannot retain his things. Tries to protect his things with violence. Leans heavily on others for his protection. His security hinges on the mechanism of violence.

Self purification and selfrealisation follow prayer and meditation. These get solidified when accompanied by fearlessness. All this is possible when an individual vanquishes the internal foes of which Gandhi spoke. In simple language the evil in man has to be driven out by the divinity in him. This is the essence of Gandhian theology.

Besides prayer and fearlessness Gandhi strongly advocated two economic concepts and could weave into a sort of religion. He presented these to his audience in theistic terms. These two are: nonpossession and bread labour. Nonstealing has a definite and distinct meaning. The meaning of nonstealing is not merely abjuring from committing theft. It means possession of things one does not require.[62] Further explaining this Gandhi pointed out that to possess something even with the permission of the owner, if one does not need it, amounts to stealing or theft. The principle of nonstealing envisages not to possess anything that one does not need. In this context Gandhi even gave the example of food.[63] It amounts to stealing if one takes a fruit one does not need it, or takes in larger quantities than necessary. According to Gandhi if an ant drags more than one grain to its ant hole amounts to theft and the meaning of stealing fits in. The essence of Gandhian declaration is that the awareness of real need puts a stop to multiplication of wants. In simple words, that multiplication of wants drives the people making themselves unconsciously thieves. Gandhi felt that poverty is the result of breaches in the principle of nonstealing. He was always of the opinion that the nature provides everything to live. The scarcity is due to stealing.

Again, Gandhi elaborated this principle of non-stealing by speaking two kinds of theft: external or physical theft and the second casting greedy eye on other's belongings. The principle of nonstealing as enunciated by Gandhi should train the individual not to think of future possession. This anxiety for the future is the root cause for many a theft. Many learned men are guilty of theft of ideas.

The entire principle of nonstealing is based on the fact that God created more than what is required for the moment. Therefore whoever appropriates more than what is required or more than his minimum wants is guilty of theft. Thus the principle of nonstealing is a pure and simple economic proposition to feed and cloth the poorest among the poors. There is nothing religion nor God in this principle. The theistic flourish and finish are there. Gandhi was adept at it: To drive home the importance of his principle to the common masses Gandhi brought God and religion on to this principle. Mainly because he had to dye it with a dye approximating this principle with theology. His audience were not intellectuals. They were the common masses seeped in theology, conservatism, orthodoxy and superstition. He had to adopt an appropriate medium. It was theistic medium. He had no time to break the impregnable shell of orthodoxy and superstition which covered the masses. He needed masses for his struggle for freedom.

Nonpossession produces a mental attitude to prepare the individual for simple life. It gives strength to cultivate a habit to reduce wants and live with simple habits. When the idea of nonpossession pushed to higher realms of Indian thought cultivation of detachment descends upon man. Every one cannot be evaluated with the same standard. To illustrate his point Gandhi always preached to have that much without which man cannot live. Similarly the detachment to body has to be developed. To Gandhi, civilization hinges not upon multiplication of wants but upon the cultivation of habits to reduce wants. Because it promotes contentment and happiness. This will have a direct bearing upon the establishment of nonviolent society.

Pushing further man into realms of ethics and moral life, Gandhi thought and applied this principle of nonpossession to thoughts. He was of the opinion that knowledge which is not necessary and removed from ethics, when becomes the point of attraction, violates the principle of nonviolence. Individual should have that knowledge which is essential to comprehend the sacredness of life on this earth. At this stage Gandhi looked to the *Gita* and wrote: "In this connection we may consider the definition of knowledge contained in the thirteenth chapter of the *Gita*. We are there told, that humility etc. constitute knowledge and all the rest is ignorance. If this is true and there is no doubt that it is true. Much that we hug today as knowledge is ignorance pure and simple and therefore only does us harm, instead of conferring any benefit. It makes the mind wander and even reduce it to vanity, and discontentment flourishes in endless ramifications of evil."[64] Further elaborating his point of view Gandhi emphasised that service to the man should occupy every moment of our life. This makes man physically active and socially purposeful. Devotion to service drives out evil activity.

From these two principles: nonpossession and nonstealing, the principle of trusteeship emerged. It is a Gandhian technique to remove exploitation from the hands of powerful and to harness in the service of man. In these two principles common civic minimum and trusteeship are clearly visible to any student of social sciences. Whenever the thought floats in the higher level metaphysics it has to be brought on to the mundane plans and conclusions have to be deducted. The Gandhian aims of service to man, removal of an exploitative hand and love and compassion will be clear.

The ultimate aim of non-possession is to emphasize the fact that man should live "not by physical strength but sufferance."[65] This leads to humility and it is the pathway to truth. At every stage brilliant ideas are deduced from the unintelligible precepts of theism to educate the man to cultivate certain mode of thinking and life to appreciate and protect sanctity of life where Gandhian Truth dances like Nataraja, the cosmic energy.

Bread labour is one of the important maxims to ameliorate the conditions of the poor. Man has the right to live only when he can earn his food by labour. This idea was dominant in Ruskin's "Unto This Last". Gandhi called this as divine law. It is purely a secular idea of economics but Gandhi clothed with a religious raiment. Taking shelter under the *Gita* Gandhi wrote : "In my view the same principle has been setforth in the third chapter of the *Gita*, where we are told, that he who eats without offering sacrifice eats stolenfood. Sacrifice here can only mean bread labour."[66] Further he took the help of the *Bible* and quoted its saying: "in the sweat of thy brow shalt thou eat thy bread." All this in simple language mean not to remain a parasite on others. Earn your food by labour. Otherwise one becomes a burden on society.

The Gandhian technique was enunciation of secular ideas and coating it with religious ideas. Again these religious sayings had to be interpreted to bring them in conformity with his original secular ideas. Thus a strong aroma of religion makes the lay amenable to these secular ideas as theistic. The result was the achievement of purpose viz. humanising the wicked and subduing the evil with divinity.

Again Gandhi went a step further and supported his line of thinking with reason. He gave an example and wrote: "A millionaire cannot carry on for long, and will soon get tired of his life, if he rolls in his bed all day long, and is even helped to his food. He, therefore, induces hunger by exercise, and helps himself to the food he eats. If every one, whether rich or poor, has thus to take exercise in some shape or form, why should it not assume the form of productive i.e. bread labour. No one asks the cultivator to take breathing exercise or to work his muscle. And more than nine-tenths of humanity lives by toil. How much happier, healthier and more peaceful would the world become, if the remaining tenth followed the example of the overwhelming majority, at least to the extent of labouring enough for the food. And many hardships connected with agriculture would be easily redressed, if such people took a hand in it. Again individual distinction of rank would be abolished, when every one without exception acknowledge the obligations of bread labour. It is common to all *Varnas*. There is worldwide conflict between capital and labour, and the poor envy the rich. If all worked for their bread, distinction of rank will be obliterated; the rich would still be there, but they would deem themselves only trustees of their property and would use it mainly in the public interest."[67] After considerable analysis and explanation, Gandhi made a distinction between a labourer and a wage slave. It is the society should encourage to do one's work even sanitary service. But society should not bind anyone to wage slavery. In all this there is nothing pertaining to God and religion. It is only an attempt to elevate man to certain heights where he can recognise divinity in men and extend his hand to help the needy struggling to life himself.

The entire chain of thought is mainly concerned how to harness man in the service of man. The twin principles, selflessness and self realisation, serve to this end. In other words it is purification of man. Only then he is fit to serve others. Humility makes the man to know his weakness as well as strength. This makes one to get himself fit to serve others. Humility makes the man to know his weakness as well as strength. This makes one to get himself fit to serve others. And he becomes an ideal instrument to cleanse society and to help the needy. Humility does not mean outward mannerism and etiquette. It is an inborn quality. Remains hidden and yet its possessor is not aware of it in him. In other words humanity is negative of egotism. "If one could erase 'I' and 'mine' from religion, politics, economics etc. he will soon be free and bring heaven on earth."[68] Once 'I' and 'mine' disappear he brings forth a life of service. Humility automatically dawns upon him. He who toils for others has hardly any time for other things. He enters into a state of selflessness and dedicates himself to the service of others.

Humility does not mean inertia as it has been in Hinduism. It is a continuous service to uphold the sanctity of life amidst death and destruction. It is a constant attempt to dedicate oneself to the service of humanity. God is ceaselessly in action without resting a moment. An individual, who gives his life every moment in the service of others, becomes a part of that momentum and action. And ultimately one feels a part of the larger whole.

Thus Gandhi understood religious concepts fully and gave to them entirely different and distinct meaning. His God is Truth. Truth is the ceaseless energy that creates life amidst death, birth, creativity and destruction. Hence protection of life demands the effort from the individual who understands sacredness of life. The momentum will remain a continuous one. Death and destruction are ever present. But if the individual is transformed into a machine towards the service of the others, not only divinity in him ignited but the divinity in others is stirred. The evil in man gets subdued. Next at a higher plane Gandhi urged the human world to respect the plant and animal life. This is possible only when man becomes selfless and realises himself. He should reduce himself to serve others. Thus his religion or *dharma* is to serve others.

REFERENCES

1. *Young India*, 11 Oct., 1928.
2. *Ibid.*
3. *Ibid.*
4. *Ibid.*
5. *Ibid.*
6. *Ibid.*
7. *In Search of the Supreme*, Vol. III, Navajivan Publishing House, Ahmedabad 1962, pp. 264 & 265.
8. *Young India*, 11 Oct., 1928.

9. *Young India,* 30 April, 1925.
10. *Young India,* 31 Dec., 1931.
11. *Ibid.*
12. *Ibid.*
13. *Ibid.*
14. *In Search of the Supreme,* Vol. II, Navajivan Publishing House, Ahmedabad, 1961, p. 72.
15. *In Search of the Supreme,* Vol. I, Navajivan Publishing House, Ahmedabad, 1961, p. 29.
16. *Op. cit.,* p. 31.
17. *Young India,* 5 June, 1924.
18. *Harijan,* 26 June, 1947.
19. *Young India,* 5 June, 1924.
20. *Ibid.*
21. *Ibid.*
22. *In Search of the Supreme,* Vol. II, Navajivan Publishing House, Ahmedabad, 1961, p. 67.
23. *Op. cit.,* p. 58, 69.
24. *Op. cit.,* p. 71.
25. *Op. cit.,* p. 72.
26. *Young India,* 20 Dec. 1928.
27. *Ibid.*
28. *Ibid.*
29. *Ibid.*
30. *Ibid.*
31. *Young India,* 20 Oct., 1926.
32. *Harijan,* 20 Oct., 1946.
33. *Young India,* 10 June, 1926.
34. *Young India,* 24 September, 1925.
35. *Ibid.*
36. *Young India,* 23 January, 1930.
37. *Ibid.*
38. *In Search of the Supreme,* Vol. I, Navajeevan Publishing House, Ahmedabad, 1961, p. 196.
39. *My Religion* : M.K. Gandhi. Editor's, Note. Navajeevan Press, Reprint, 1985, p. (iii).
40. *Prayer* : M.K. Gandhi, National Publishing House, Ahmedabad, Second Ed, 1984, p. 172.
41. *Ibid.*
42. *Op. cit.,* p. 173.
43. *Op. cit.,* p. 177 (*Young India,* 22 January 1925).
44. *Young India,* 4 April 1929.

45. *Harijan*, 22 June 1946.
46. *Young India*, 27 October, 1927.
47. *Young India*, 25 April, 1929.
48. *Ibid*.
49. *Ibid*.
50. Iravati Karve, *Youganta*: *The End of An Epoch*, Sangam Books, New Delhi, 1974, p. 7.
51. *Young India*, 10 September, 1942.
52. *Harijan*, 1 Feb., 1942.
53. *Harijan*, 2 November, 1925.
54. M.K. Gandhi : *Ashram Observances in Action*, Navajivan Publishing House, Ahmedabad, Second Print (First Edition 1955, pp. 18 to 21).
55. *Op. cit.*, p. 147.
56. *In Search of the Supreme*, Vol. II, p. 60.
57. *Ibid*.
58. *In Search of the Supreme*, Vol. II, pp. 60, 61.
59. *Ibid*.
60. *Ibid*.
61. *Op. cit.*, p. 62.
62. *In Search of the Supreme*, Vol. II, p. 102.
63. *Ibid*.
64. *In Search of the Supreme*, Vol. II, p. 107.
65. *Young India*, 5 February, 1925.
66. *In Search of the Supreme*, Vol. II, p. 113.
67. *In Search of the Supreme*, Vol. II, pp. 113 & 114.
68. *Young India*, 23 September, 1926.

4

Was Gandhi A Mystic?

FAITH and wisdom dominate theology. It gets sustenance from faith and wisdom: In religion faith rules the lives of men. It is because man puts faith on certain reality. But the evidence to this reality is not seen. Religion acts as evidence to reality. Hence where there is religion there is faith. On faith alone religion thrives. In short "faith is the substance of things hoped for, the evidence of the things is not seen."[1] It is religion that provides evidence. Hope leads to living. Faith generates hope, unevidenced reality shrouded in religion draws faith and kindles hope. This reality either provides moral armour to the man or becomes a sword for fanaticism in his hand.

The teaching of religion is that faith leads to wisdom. As and when faith provides moral armour to man he starts believing certain principles of life and lives with conviction. This faith leads the individual to the path of wisdom. The human life that generally considered "fugitive and fragile" gets strength and meaning. He finds meaning to his life. Where consciousness is wider and deep, enlightenment descends upon certain people. Like the Buddha in some cases it becomes an instrument to remove the devil in man or to texture a social fabric to eliminate exploitation. Thus in both the cases harmony in society is maintained. Friction will be the least if not purged altogether. On the other hand when faith becomes a sword, fanaticism oozes out. Consequences are as clear as crystal.

The Hebrew Bible says "the fear of the Lord leads to wisdom." In religion faith presupposes wisdom. Hence a distinction has to be made between the wisdom of the philosopher and of the prophet. The philosopher looks into the value of man and thinks with certain amount of introspection and reasoning. Man can look inwards to recognise his capability for enlightenment. This was the line of reasoning that Gandhi adopted and believed in the divinity in man. A prophet injects inputs in the name of unevidenced reality in man and tries to improve the moral strength in a fragile body. Somewhere in mid imperceptible zone of these two Gandhi stood. Some think that Gandhi was nearer to the zone of prophet's domain. These people are scared to look at Gandhi anything but a rationalist if not atheist. This resulted into millions of words like religion, God and faith that covered and clothed Gandhi. To the others who looked at Gandhi for inspiration to action and selfless service, felt that Gandhi was nearer to the domain of the philosopher. To them Gandhi was a philosopher and a politician par-excellence. Their appreciation of Gandhi was critical. It was not adoration, it was critical appreciation. In them traces of rationalism and agnosticism are found.

In the Indian setting any attempt to bring out rationalist explanation in the *Vedas*, the *Upanishads* and epics amounts to sacrilege. The result is unqualified panegyric of our legend and lore. Any critical appreciation by any one has been frowned. One writer interpreted *Mahabharata* as "all human efforts are fruitless and all human life ends in frustration."[2] This is a great revelation. It gives a reader an opportunity to get himself mirrored. He learns. It helps to view one's life critically. Introspection enables to lead a healthy life. Whereas a revivalist looks at *Mahabharata* as a book of virtue and truth to be followed every moment. Self indulgence depicted by the princes in *Mahabharata* was their ruin. Thus revivalist culture demands the people to believe everything that was written in our scriptures, and urges to follow moral guide lines to achieve what Hinduism considers supreme. This binds the individual to the iron frame of moral code in religion. He cannot lead a life of content and comfort. The fear of this moral code makes the individual to renounce creative thinking and action.

Scientific interpretation of Gandhi's view on religion, God and prayer is of utmost importance when brought into the context of struggle for freedom. It gives an idea how this 'Godstunt' served as motive force and gave momentum to battles. In this struggle Gandhi has to be brought on to the Indian setting and viewed. Otherwise the flake of religious cover may not fall. The mysticism that surrounded his thought remains covering reality.

In the Indian setting every movement when gets a coat of moralist colour slips into religion. The mighty *Vedas* and the lofty

Upanishads make every movement as a religious one. Every movement gradually slides from the twilight zone of philosophy into the twilight zone of religion. Similar was the fate of the Gandhian thought. Entire Gandhian thought vis-a-vis religion got a religious coat rather thick from the interpreters of Gandhi's ideas on religion and God. To pull out the Gandhian thought from this rut and put it afresh requires thorough understanding of the political, social and historical currents through which Gandhi had passed. Again one has to visualise how these factors influenced Gandhi. And what was the aim of Gandhi?

Now the question is what is Indian setting? In the religious context to be more precise in the realm of philosophy-cum-theology any writer or a thinker who leans more on to the side of philosophy may be side tracked. Very often he may be considered a rationalist if not an atheist or a heretic. This deprives him of adulation and admiration, love and affection. He cannot get these from the masses. Though Gandhi leaned more on philosophy he kept the balance holding on to the ropes of religion. Consequently the philosophic reality remained hidden.

Indian lives in eternity. Speculation in philosophy coevolved with the birth of culture and civilization. It is a continuous process and never ends. The *Vedas* true knowledge of philosophy sprouted on Indian soil some five thousand years ago, still inspire human mind to speculate over truth. Things are being still reinterpreted and reanalysed to know the truth. The *Vedanta* is the end of the attainment of knowledge.[3] The *Vedantic* belief is that high souled sages moving from place to place purified the whole earth. They sanctified the *teerthas*.[4] This sort of view dominates the Indian philosophy and the Hindu theology. Everything gets a wash of religion. Periodic reinforcement of religion takes place and consequently theological dominance gets solidified.

The emergence of rationalism and liberalism made to germinate intellectual pursuits. Throughout history attempt to separate intellectual pursuits from philosophy is evident. The latter as understood in the west is unknown in India. From a cultural point of view the philosophical systems of Plato and Aristotle in ancient period and in modern period the system emanated from the writings of Kant and Hegel, if studied without any bias, lead to wonderful understanding of man, whereas philosophy in India looked beyond the humanbeing.

The importance of intellectual values for the uplift of human comfort dominated. While the mighty current of the Indian philosophy in the realms of the *Vedas* and the *Upanishads* turned to *Atman* and subsequently towards universal religion. The concept of *Atman* became the object of philosophical speculation. Refinement of soul at every stage of birth envisioned. And thus refinement of human being and human life became speculation of philosophy. At a lower level i.e. at the level of the priest and the preacher Indian philosophy became the synonym of *Maya, Karma and Tyaga*. At a higher level the refinement of humanbeing touched the theological concepts of universal religion. Gradually because of intellectual values, liberalism the bed rock of human development and the system of thought that concerned with restructuring of human society attracted. In Indian philosophy restructuring of society does not find any importance, whereas refinement of humanbeing dominates. At the same time Indian philosophy does not speak of any inputs to inject into man.

Philosophy is defined as a search for truth. At this stage truth should not be confused with universal truth or ultimate truth. In this context truth is to know the human environs and also truth about cosmos. Till today science is on the periphery of truth. It has not yet penetrated into the inner core so far. Hence speculation for truth persists. In our country this entire thought was and even today is towards the pacification of man and his final refinement, but not towards restructuring society to eliminate exploitation. Purification and restructuring of man has been the urge of Indian thought. This enabled the emergence of *Atman*. It is more or less a carrier to refine man. Removal of beast in man is a possibility through the agency of soul. This is the main theme of Indian Philosophy. Gandhi was all for the refinement of man. But his approach was different. He did not depend upon the mechanism and speculation of soul. His aim and method were different. His aim was to turn the man to look into himself. His method was nonviolence. i.e. holding on to truth *Satyagraha* and win the heart of the opponent. In simple words it is to stir the divinity in one's opponent and take him out from the path of evil. Therefore Gandhi never appeared as a mystic. He was a man of action. Results satisfied him. He never remained in the layers of speculation.

Philosophy is a constant attempt to know truth. While awareness of soul is mainly and solely possible through experience. It is the direct experience that makes one to grasp and understand the concept of soul in theology and philosophy. Apart from the refinement of soul, man improves spiritually under the guidance of a *Guru* or a mystic. At this stage he experiences a sort of bliss in the beginning. At a bit higher stage one experiences emancipated bliss. Gandhi saw divinity in man. Felt this divinity and always remained determined that divinity in man can be stimulated to put him on the right path of good. Gandhi himself never tried to experience the bliss which a mystic experiences. He did not want to be guided or helped by any *Guru*. He never wanted to search religion for enlightened bliss. He was attracted to persons like Raichandbhai, Tolstoy and Ruskin because of their intellect and moral earnestness. According to Gandhi these three are not perfect *Jnanis*. Nor Gandhi wanted to become a perfect *Jnani* where faith and wisdom in right proportions get mixed up. Gandhi was not on the path of a mystic. Hence there was no search for *guru* in him.[5]

The concept of emancipated bliss is beyond the human comprehension, because beauty of the soul cannot be conceived from the planes of mind. This understanding leads to the understanding of the distinction between the soul and the mind. Mind takes to a particular point. Beyond that mind cannot peep into reality. Hope and wisdom take the man to a point to see the reality of soul. At this point mysticism descends. Gandhi never attempted even to reach this point.

In Indian philosophical speculation a distinction between mind and soul is made. The latter has been declared as superior to mind. This leads to light and enlightenment. In this light and enlightenment mystic walks. He is more pronounced in the Hindu milieu. Importance of a mystic has been fully recognised in the Hindu ethos. His or her presence is vital to improve humanbeings and to sanctify the places. Mystic strives for effecting union with the ultimate reality. In the realm of theology mystic has a unique place. It is because he leads the man to a light which he has never imagined. In Gandhian matrix there is no room for mysticism and mystic. Gandhi strove to improve the moral fibre in man and make him an ideal *Satyagrahi*. His aim was to effect revolution and removal of exploitation. He never aimed for union with universal truth. Neither he urged the masses to look into this aspect.

While discussing with the intellectual in the west, or more precisely encountering with the west, our mystics and students of philosophy make a distinction between philosophical speculation and intellectual values. The latter belong mostly to the west. Philosophy and intellectual values can be understood and can be properly analysed for the benefit of the lay by reasoning alone. But, while what is beyond philosophy is too illusive to be grasped by the ordinary people. It is because what is beyond philosophy has to be experienced to be understood. The play of faith and wisdom will be full. Gandhi's faith lies in the goodness of man. His wisdom was his creed of nonviolence as the operating principle to effect change in society to mellow society. The rigours of living get softened.

The word *Atman* is a close approximation to soul. Correct understanding of the word soul needs to uncover illusion surrounding the concept of soul. With the emergence of science, scientific enquiry emerged. Many things have been debunked by scientific enquiry including the concept of soul as understood in the realm of philosophy. Mind with its intuition, divination and other things draws out many things from the subconscious and subliminal state. But what exactly soul constitutes is difficult to be perceived and put in words. The distinctive attributes of soul are still illusive to mind. To this limitation the Indian mystic explains that mind is not guide to escort the man from the alleys of darkness to light. It is the mystic experience that guides towards enlightenment. This experience tantalizes the individual. It is called *aparoksha anubhuti*. This tantalizing experience touches every aspect of human body, knowledgeable mind, heart and eyes. This vision is all embracing, skies and oceans too. It touches everything in nature. This makes limitation of mind apparent. This soul vision is beyond the capability of mental theorising.

Mind and reasoning cannot put the individual beyond horizon giving an idea of the vision of a mystic. Reasoning results into doctrine dominated by repulsion and fear. These doctrines are attempts to remove fear, repulsion and human suffering by redesigning society. Redesigning of society is a continuous effort. To this end secular doctrines and theories are propounded. While the attempt to refine the individual falls within the purview of the soul vision.

Mental vision takes the individual to a certain extent. But, still curiosity in man pushes him to see beyond mental vision. Scientific enquiry does not satisfy the individual. He feels and thinks that the scientific enquiry does not dispel the illusions around certain aspect where mental vision is of no use. Because of this curiosity he takes the help of those who could see beyond mental vision. At this stage slowly and imperceptibly this vision opens up to man. Soul vision gradually but slowly emerges. Man, when breaks the mental shell, leads himself to more freedom. He begins to see "unknown modes of being". In this context Gandhian perception of *Satya* and *Ahimsa* slowly emerge. The master design of refining individual as Gandhi perceived becomes more clear.

Once the mental shells are broken limitations of man crumble. He will be able to see gradually spiritual reality. This spiritual reality is the dawn of religion. It is *dharma*. It is the craving to see harmony in the maker's creation. Appreciation of this harmony follows later. Gandhi could perceive the energy and the rhythm of the movement in the universe. He felt it. He could not see. This rhythm and movement in the universe is the truth for Gandhi. He calls this truth as God or *vice versa*.

Bioengineering, space exploration, communication marvel, super computers over super computers, shield against atomic annihilation etc. are the signs of the triumph of mind. At the same time this success of mind pushed the man on to the path of the truth. In other words the marvel when tried to control the forces of nature the balance in nature disturbed with far reaching ill effects on man. This makes the man to try to see what is truth. At this stage the hand of mystic is necessary to him. Dispassionate teaching of science proved the achievement of mind. The control of nature is not achieved by soul. Mind can disturb the balance in nature. Hence it has to be controlled. And this control should be the control of soul over mind. Because, as long as mind is under the control of man, it serves best. The Indian ethos demands the obedience of mind to soul. Once mind gets intoxicated with success mental ego breeds hatred and contempt. Man's greed gets satisfied with the progress of controlling nature. But the profit that emanates from the success of the mind gets dissipated early. The higher values of man get less importance. Mundane things get precedence against the values of soul. The harmony that is in existence gets shattered. But the beauty is that the maker cannot be deceived. He has given liberty to the individual to fashion his life. If he is careful and less greedy the evolution goes on more or less perfectly. And he becomes a better being. Thus the liberty is in the hands of the individual either to devote himself to become a better humanbeing or to suffer from the dreaded disease of mental ego.

"Mysticism is not merely an imaginative thought about nature or about its forces or an emotional upsurge concerned more with the feelings than with the reality, that constitutes mysticism."[6] Thus mysticism is there in a saint but different from his body and emotion and feeling. It is concerned with the reality to which a mystic looks at and sees soul vision. In the case of Gandhi he had not reached a stage where he can view the reality as a mystic and remain silent appreciating the enlightened bliss and very often sunk in this bliss. Like any thinker Gandhi's goal was clear. He enunciated and declared his aim as truth. Sometimes felt that he could not explain what is truth. The rhythm and movement of the universe has the energy. And this energy Gandhi felt. Feeling of this reality brings Gandhi on to the door step of becoming a mystic.

A few will be able to see some faint glimpse through the chinks in mental shells. And the mystic has a social purpose to reform the man. He tries to educate the lay through his example. His main thrust is to show the multitude the way for harmony in nature and thereby to achieve harmony in society. The result will be a friction free harmonious existence. The true meaning of the word mysticism derived from the Greek word '*mustein*'.[7] It means to close ones lips. So mysticism is a philosophy and if it is pushed further it means realisation of God and enjoyment of God in silence. Wherever it is to be found whether in Christianity, or in Islam or in Hinduism it is called mysticism or philosophy of *Mauna*. This stage of realisation of reality is not found in Gandhi. His enjoyment was not the bliss of the soul vision. His enjoyment was in refining the individual. Only when he could stir the divinity in man for the betterment of life, Gandhian aim was consummated.

The average Indian and the men who take to the preaching of Indian thought and religion feel that the soul vision is a gift to a very few at the dawn of Indian civilization. This bright vision was darkened in course of time. It will be visible to those who patiently think over the purpose of life at a ripe age. Their sole mission is to know the human life. They try to get out of this cloud of darkness. And it is a part of cosmic play. One cannot have a soul vision unless one craves for it over all other things. It cannot be one among the things one needs it. Gandhi's aim not confined to see this vision of reality. He was primarily a rebel, a revolutionary and a nonconformist. His aim was to ameliorate the conditions of the poor. It was not through mystic experience but through a programme of action.

A mystic always opts for silence. He is a God realiser. Sits silent and does not speak. He does not utter any word at all. His enjoyment lies in the appreciation of the creation and working of God within himself. To describe God or reality by a word of mouth is impossible. Real experience of it is in the heart. Thus the structure of mysticism and the aim of mystic are clear. Gandhi never contemplated on these lines. Gandhi's emphasis on heart brings him on to the path of mystic. Beyond that Gandhi was never a mystic. Mysticism never overshadowed him.

A sceptic doubts about the advisability of craving for soul vision over all other things. The fruit of todays material progress say whether the progress of science or the achievement of mind is the result of human relentless endeavour passing through adventure, discovery, invention, failure and success, toil, blood and tears. Even with all this, the world based on mind is crumbling. Slowly we are reaching the dead end. Therefore soul vision is essential. It pushes the man into a state of fearlessness, and annihilation of hatred. Otherwise man exercises the right to suicide. In the Gandhian idiom *Satyagraha* and nonviolence are crying need of man for his very survival on this earth. It is because fear lingers in human relations. Mind does not contribute towards the strength of man. It breeds more fear. Scepticism rules the mind. This brings fear. And fear leads to hatred.

Soul vision makes man to see God. He will be facing God face to face. Takes orders from him alone. Gets guidance from him. Sees everything in this reality. At this stage Hindu theology merges with Indian philosophy. Intellectual values look feeble and worthless. The people who claim that they are with God face to face exploit the individual. The gullible and credulous fall prey to them. Once exploitation becomes the accepted norm these *Mahants* judge the man not as a man. He is judged with colour of religion in which he is born. In this twilight zone between the soul vision and theology Gandhi stood. He refused to be drawn into the fold of theology nor could he go far towards the soul vision, because of his mission to lift the masses from ignorance and exploitation. He was fighting a political battle. He was alive to the grim-realities in Indian situation. Because of this pull he remained occupied with day-to-day affairs of his masses.

Now the question is: How to identify the soul? This question emerges from the fact that mind alone knows the things. The concept of soul is a myth. It is because intellectual dialectics start with doubt and scepticism. The climate of doubt is created. To mind soul is a myth. Mind cannot delve deep to fathom soul. One gets into the mould what one constantly thinks. The *Gita* speaks of this. At one stage discussing *Brahmacharya* Gandhi had said that if one always thinks of incest he will be guilty of incest. Thus the thought ultimately culminates into action. The ordinary masses believe in the existence of soul and the thought connected with the soul. While the intellectual lives in doubt. Doubts the existence of soul. Therefore the masses are called weak and dumb. The Christ called the masses as 'weak'. This weak and meek who live by faith see the soul. While the intelligentia despises the weak, Gandhi drew strength from the weak. His passion was to involve the weak in the struggle for freedom. He was successful.

The concept of soul vision to the intelligentia remained always a sort of fanaticism against reason. Whereas the masses have faith in the soul vision of a mystic, the latter always feels that soul vision is a reality. The masses believe by associating with mystics they can see and experience something of the vision which is the sole concern of a mystic. Are the mystics really available? If they are in existence how many are they? Their number is too small. At the most a couple of them. They are venerated souls on the Indian soil. They are a part of the Indian ethos and the Indian philosophy. In the Indian culture there is craving to get associated with mystics to have a glimpse of soul vision if one is fortunate. This craving for soul vision prevented India from degeneration and disintegration. She had her sustenance from the reverence she had been showing to the spiritual values that had grown on its soil. To the ordinary masses Gandhi had this aura, though he never attempted to lead a life of a mystic. His mysticism was his faith in the masses. His aim was different from the aim of a mystic. He never talked the language of mystics. He made his conception of religion and God clear to himself.

A mystic's sole aim is to liberate the man from the mundane things of the world. Turn the latter's eye towards spiritual values. The spiritual values as seen by Gandhi are different from the spiritual values which a mystic cherishes. The liberation which a mystic tries involves, firstly change in the mode of living. In other words he thrives on the minimum things necessary for existence. Rest of his effort goes to the service of the people. Secondly, it is examination and retrospection of attachment to the existing mode of life. He sees a higher aim or purpose of life. The things that one feels essential for the present mode of life are secondary to a mystic. His attachment is not towards the material things of life. His attachment is with beautiful vision of the unseen. He craves for it. He discards everything. His attempt in the search for the human existence remains always with him. Thirdly, a mystic's liberation is the realisation to shed attachment. In his search for the meaning of life he realises to get himself detached with material objects. Renunciation becomes a norm with him. He gets bliss in renouncing things. Gandhi advocated renouncing and detachment to make the individual fit to render selfless service to others. Whereas a mystic feels that he would be able to experience bliss only when there is total detachment from material things. Fourthly, liberation is possible only when one is able to get a *Guru* who had got rid of attachment. Gandhi never preached for a *Guru* nor did he try to become a disciple of any individual however great he might be. Neither he did become a *Guru*. He advocated detachment from material things and enjoyment in renunciation. For this he felt that a *Guru* was not required. He oriented the masses to give their best to their fellow beings. Fifthly, and lastly reaching to a *Guru* is the cardinal principle to achieve liberation. Gandhi appreciated the association of *Guru* to escort a *chela*. But he never wanted a *Guru*. Nor did he feel the necessity of *Guru*. Further Gandhi thought that an ideal *Guru* is not available. To make an ordinary average individual as an instrument in service of man does not require that much of spiritual discipline which a mystic demands from his disciple. The mystic wants to make his disciple a spiritual being to get liberated from the existing mode of life. Even service to his fellow being is not of that higher order similar to the liberation which the concept of soul envisages. All these five aspects have to be thoroughly examined to know the meaning of human existence vis-a-vis Gandhi's aim of human life. To Gandhi truth lives in the sacredness of life, whether it is human, animal or plant. Creation takes place amidst destruction. Life persists amidst death. Nonviolence forms the oily film between the two surfaces. Exploitation and friction are removed by nonviolence. *Satyagraha* is the sole aim. While a mystic in the path to liberation takes away the individual from the existing mode of life and makes the individual misfit for normal existence.

A mystic feels that it is very easy to reach a wise man. Soul craves to be associated with the wise. It is the sceptic mind stands in the way. It suspects the wise. Frowns and scorns the wise. The result is that the spiritual values in the individual do not get nourished. For the enrichment of spiritual values faith and wisdom are necessary. Reason becomes futile. It cannot liberate the mind from scepticism. Not only Gandhi recognised these spiritual values but took cognizance to the limitation of reasoning. At this stage Gandhi is totally different from a mystic. The latter does not see man as a man with all his limitations. He feels that these limitations can be wiped out. Once these limitations are rectified the individual will be on the path to liberation and can enjoy bliss, the ultimate aim of human existence. On the other hand Gandhi recognised these spiritual values. He did not pursue liberation of man. He wanted to harness these spiritual values in man to serve his fellow men better. The quantum of good in man constitutes spiritual values. These positive qualities in man have to be utilised in politics and for social reforms. The masses had to be brought into politics to end colonialism and to reform society and man within. Certain aspects of Gandhi remained invisible to the lay as well as intelligentsia. Hence the mystic hue on him still lingers.

In India the saint and the mystic strove for the self liberation. They were loved and adored by the ruler as well as the ruled. This phenomenon was evident throughout the history. Whatever upheavals took place both in the ancient and medieval periods people had love for a saint and a seer who had the gift of the soul vision. Even in the midst of suffering i.e. war and poverty the mystic showed light and kindled hope in the masses for wisdom. This kept the Indian ethos unsullied and intact. India is a long continuum in this respect. It is yet to be seen with the craving for material civilization. The Indian ethos and culture will remain the same or change seeking justification for everything it craves in the days to come. If we look at Gandhi from this angle his preaching for selfless service has a meaning and a potential principle for guidance and correction.

The contact with the west, an erroneous notion has been implanted in the minds of the intelligentsia that the downfall of India was due to over emphasis on the pursuit of spiritual side of the human life, very often Jawaharlal Nehru, a positivist and agnostic in the eyes of the west was always equated as saying that the caste system was mainly responsible for the integration of our country and the perpetuation of our ethos. He never supported the degraded form of caste as it is degenerated now. Similarly when M.N. Roy declared that the entire Hindu society is the church of the Hindus he was referring to the impact of spiritual values on the Hindu society distinct from the temple and the priest. This all embracing quality of the Hindu spiritual life over the Hindu mind, culture and ethos made those who look at India think that India lives in eternity. Spiritual values liberated the average masses from materialism. No doubt people near the seats of power, and with power and pelf say the prince and the priest got immersed with materialism. But contamination of materialism did not have much impact on the masses. This refusal to accept the Godless materialism helped Indian to survive through millenniums even when long spells of anarchy prevailed in the country. During these periods she remained emaciated. But the spiritual values nourished the soul. Hence reverence and respect for tradition and spiritual ethos lingered. India believed in the fact that even a single mystic will serve as the saviour of whole generation. In this context it is highly relevant to know whether Gandhi had become a mystic or not. Evidence is to the contrary.

Close associates of Gandhi believed the aura around Gandhi was due to his mysticism.[8] To them Gandhi's spiritual experience began from very early in life and culminated towards the end of his career. Those who observed Gandhi from this angle trace three stages in him. The first stage about the inner voices which he had been uttering. It was compared to *Ananta*, sound of mystical experience. The second stage indicated the message he received from the inner voice. He had never made it clear what the message was. The third stage was his declaration of message. Prof. R.D. Ranade illustrated this in the following way:

> "We shall begin by considering that the first stage is historical perspective. In the year 1921 we have got an utterance from Mahatma Gandhi telling us that he heard the still small voice and also that he saw a pillar of fire. Normally he says, man shuts his ears to the one and the eyes to the other. If we collected together mystical experience of Mahatma Gandhi we might say on the whole that he was an audible rather than a photic of morphist. Not that he had no experience of Inner Light. But he tells us that the inner light must be supported by the voice of God and then alone it may become effective. In the year 1924 we are told by him that he claimed no prophethood. That he yearned to see God face to face. We also learn from him that the whole of his activity was directed to that end ethical, social, political and humanitarian. In the year 1925 he speaks of the virtue of dancing to the tune of the flute *(Bansuri)*, exhorting people that if they were fortunate to hear this all would be well with them. In the year 1933 we are told by Mahatma Gandhi that the inner voice has become audible. This is as much as to say that the inner voice having started from a small beginning assumed greater and greater sonorousness and power as time rolled on. In the year 1936 we have a general reflection of his to the effect that this divine music constantly going on inside us, only very few are able to listen to it. It is just because human senses drown the delicate music, that men are unable to hear it. He however tells us that he who rises superior to the senses can hear the voice of God. Gandhi tells us that this sound is going on incessantly in us, in that matter imitating Shankaracharya who spoke about the resonance of inner conscience. Finally we are told by Gandhi that this divine music is infinitely superior to any thing that we can hear by means of our senses."[9]

What was the craving of a mystic in Mahatma Gandhi? There are three stages : Conscience, the divinity in man and the recognition of heeding to the dictates of the divinity in man. The social purpose of his scheme is very clear. He had always striven in this direction. Whenever in doubt he knocked at the door of divinity in man. Thus he was guided. His experiments of Truth were in this direction. He spoke religion, God, faith and wisdom to suit to the frame in which nonviolence and *Satyagraha* leading to Truth takes place. This gave him a quasi religious complexion. He was more than a political activist. To his follower and opponent he was looked less as a politician and rebel but more as a representative of spiritual values embedded in religion, though he never appreciated religion and its preacher. If at all Gandhi appreciated religion it is when these ideas strengthen his operative principle of nonviolence and the pursuit of truth.

There is never a conflict between the reason the supreme gift of man and the appreciation to thrive for soul vision. Man is gifted with liberty unhindered to move whichever way he likes. He is free to move in any direction he likes. He is free to preach atheism if he feels that it will deliver goods he requires. Similarly a theist feels assured to put faith in God. Here Gandhi's position is very simple and straight: the possession of love, faith, humanity and submission. And he believes always that he can make man cross the Rubicon. The saint or a mystic neither covets knowledge nor power to lead the world. He just prays for the right path and soul vision, inner strength and to see God Almighty. In India the saint never told that people should believe in God. He only educated the people in the ways of God. And ultimately succeeded to make his follower God believer. This position can be illustrated from the relation between Ramakrishna Paramhansa and his disciple Vivekananda. God never appears to the mind of reason. It is only through personal experience one believes in God. God's ways may be inscrutable but effective. If this measuring rod or frame of reasoning applied to Gandhi somewhat a different picture emerges. He had knowledge. At every stage he took the help of reason to judge the things. He was not a blind believer and not a blind follower. Intellectuals of his age approached him for guidance. He never coveted power. At the same time moulded the thought of his followers. He came very close to a point to be fully recognised as a saint. Yet, he remained at the threshold of a saint or a mystic. The pull towards politics was more forceful. He was a politician, a rebel, and a social reformer. He was more secular than theological. He was more rational than intuitional.

To a trained mind fantasy, hallucinations phantoms and extra sensory perceptions never appeal. A mystic who does not take the help of mind sees vision through experience. This becomes the medium to experience reality. This kind of reality to reason is fantasy. It is like the reality of an ignorant. It is the fantasy of a knowledgeable. The superior and deeper consciousness of a sage gives him vision for which he starves. Thus a gulf is formed between the mystic and the moral. This gulf remains always between the two unabridged. Always two view points emerge. Gandhi was being in the imperceptible twilight zone of the two could not see much of the vision. Gandhi took the help of the reason and worked for the uplift of the poor, and finally for the removal of friction in society. Had he seen the vision with which a mystic is familiar he would have educated the masses in a different way. His reference points in his march would have been different.

This soul vision makes a man a superior man or a better man. A better man means moral values in the human context. But moral values are different from spiritual values. A mystic aims at spiritual values through his superior consciousness. He was not concerned with moral values. Moral values are byproducts of the pursuit of spiritual values. To that extent alone a mystic helps for the development of moral values in man. Ethics are the first steps in the pursuit of spiritual values. Moral values give thrust for higher flight into spiritual values. Now turning to science, scientific knowledge no doubt improves the material comfort of the people. But it cannot guarantee moral values. Whereas spiritual values guarantee moral values. Gandhi at the door step of mysticism turned to moral values refusing to move further towards spiritual direction. He used the symbol and the language of spiritual values to improve man and dragged him to political arena. A mystic stakes everything for spiritual values. To him heart and soul are important than mind. Gandhi looked at the masses and tried to improve the masses inculcating the spirit of heart and soul; but refused to go further for any enlightenment. His conception of enlightenment is already predetermined. It is simple and mundane yet difficult to achieve. Unless the heart and soul have become ruling passion, one cannot become a mystic.

Mystics are always compassionate, understanding, tolerant, forgiving, pure hearted, kind, chaste and loving. But these qualities are not found even though one is most moralistic and humanitarian. Mystics like Buddha, Christ, St. Francis, St. Theresa, St. Augustine, St. Bernast, Jacob Boehme, Fra Angelo, Echast, Ryjsbrock, Sri Chaitanya, Mira Bai, Sri Ramakrishna are the striking examples who had staked their lives for enlightenment.

People who have commented upon the mystic quality of Gandhi gave two incidents in Gandhi's life when he reached pinnacle of his experience in spiritual values. They think that Gandhi heard the mystical voice on two occasions.[10] But people who were near him were neither aware of the sound nor the substance. These two occasions were; one in 1940 and the other in 1948. In the year 1940 in the course of anti-war propaganda by nonviolent means Mahatma Gandhi had a resolution placed before the All India Congress Committee. He tried for some time but without any success before the members. But he was absolutely confident about its veracity and communicated to others as it was a command from the inner voice. Gandhi said, "The thing I have placed before you is not small. I myself had thought it was small. But it was not so. It has not come from my intellect. It has come from the recess of heart where dwelth inner most. It is He who has given it. It has born at the end of travail."[11]

In this statement most of the associates could easily see religious tenor and could easily identify Gandhi with a mystic. But if one analyses keeping Gandhi's meaning of God and religion, the statement was not all that mystic in colour and content. Gandhi was the ardent supporter of nonviolence and his God was Truth. His truth reflects the energy behind the momentum in the nature. He was against war. He did not support the war. A man like Jawaharlal Nehru did not see any religion or any mystic-call in it. But he weighed it in political terms and supported Gandhi saying : "How great Mahatma Gandhi spiritually is, I cannot say, I can tell you that he is politically without a peer". Thus he hinted at political advantage with moral backing.

On another occasion some writers attribute divine communication was in the year 1948 just before his earthly career came to an end. Gandhi wanted to go on fast to bring the desired result in the heart of the Hindu as well as the Muslim. He wanted to stop the fratricidal war. He wanted to sacrifice his life rather than to become a witness to the "mindless killings". He said on this occasion. "There are friends who do not believe in the method of the fast for the reclamation of the human mind . . . . with God as my supreme and sole counsellor. I felt that I must take the decision without any other advisor. If I have made a mistake and discovered it, I shall have no hesitation in proclaiming it from the house top and retracing my faulty step. There is little chance making such a discovery. If there is a clear indication as I claim there is, the Inner voice it will not be gain said. I plead for all absence of argument and inevitable endorsement of the step . . . . I urge everybody dispassionately to examine the purpose and leave me die, if I must in peace . . . . death for me would be glorious deliverance rather than that I should be a helpless witness of the destruction of India, Hinduism, Sikhism and Islam."[12] These two declarations one in 1940 and the second in 1948 are purely to vindicate nonviolence. The latter one was essentially to uphold his life's mission. A man who dedicated his life for nonviolence and who could see the inner unity of religions could not but stop the communal riots at the cost of his life. The associates of Gandhi who remained with him in *Asram*, both at Sabarmati and Wardha saw religion in Gandhi. Every turn in him has been interpreted in terms of theology. To them the spiritual veil over Gandhi was too heavy to be lifted easily.

A mystic never speaks till he knows. Only when his knowledge is complete he will speak of the concepts like bliss and enlightenment. He gets satisfied first and then only ventures to speak to his followers. It is not preaching. It is an attempt to turn the inward eye to scan himself. Therefore mystic experience pre-supposes arduous self-discipline. Through this rigorous self-discipline for self purification larger consciousness involves. Thus he gets a deep and extensive knowledge of the occult and spiritual forces. Gandhi had passed through rigorous self-discipline. Perfected himself to follow nonviolence and to hold on to truth. He was a perfect *Satyagrahi*. But he was not a mystic. His self-discipline was directed towards political battles against colonialism and social reform movement. Therefore his self-disciplining effort though flawless, larger consciousness never evolved in him. The bliss which is a reality in the life of mystic remained illusive to Gandhi. Moreover Gandhi never tried to become a mystic.

Like scientific knowledge, spiritual knowledge too, does not place primary importance on morals. Moral improvement takes place in an individual automatically as a by-product when he is on the path towards spiritual values. A genuine mystic never aims at his moral development to become a better man. On the contrary, the sole aim in a mystic is to see God within himself. His main aim is the attainment of enlightenment and the understanding of the universe. He has to recognise the place of man in the universe. Whereas pursuit of morals looks at the improvement of man and the improvement of his environment i.e. society. It has two aspects. First it is the improvement of man i.e. purification of man. In terms o social sciences it means restructuring the individual. Proper input have to be made into an effective instrument in the removal of evi in man and consequently exploitation in society. Gandhi strove t this end. Second aspect is to restructure society by removing that par in society which becomes the main propellant for exploitation. Thi aspect leads to doctrinaire approach like socialism, communism an pluralism. The Gandhian approach is to ask the individual to hol on to Truth : *Satyagraha*. This brings the best in man, and help towards the removal of exploitation and misery. The importance c Gandhi lies in the improvement of the individual and society Everything is to be restructured on the basis of morals. Nonviolenc supplies oily film between various parts of society to remove frictio Social relations will be a smooth flow. The political ideologi primarily aim at reforming society thinking that the individual incapable of moulding himself. On the contrary Gandhi believed th though it is difficult to bring about necessary change in the individu he is the centre of society. He has to be reformed at the outset. A amount of change in social structure because of innovation economics and science society cannot improve the individual. It the individual who can bring out changes in social relation, on when he is improved.

A mystic is concerned with heart and soul. Only when it become his only mission he becomes a mystic. Because of his concern wit heart and soul it leads to compassion, understanding, toleranc forgiveness, pure heart, kindness, chastity and love. These were the hallmarks in all the mystics from the Buddha to Rama Krishna. Any limitation in these leads the so called mystics as preachers and propagandists. The contemporary 'God Men' prevalent on our soil are the living examples.

In India the common man places faith in mystics. He adores him. Tradition continues. India has remained India. She radiates faith where even doubts linger. This guides the people a chosen few to the discovery of the Supreme. Before this the material world remains incomplete, feeble and pale. Realisation lingers on faith. This faith leads the people towards the Supreme Being. But a faith which does not lead to any where is meaningless. It is an effort without fruit. Faith gradually leads to realisation. Once divine vision is visible to him, a mystic becomes more fastidious than an intellectual or a rationalist and even a scientist. He is even ambitious. This ambition is to see God clearly. In these qualities where did Gandhi stand? Like a mystic he was fastidious and ambitious. It was a contiguous craving to know the common man on this soil. Because of his understanding of the common man his technique facilitated him to involve the masses in his battle against colonialism, communalism and towards social reform. He could make them aware of the sacredness of life.

In our country mystic remained silent towards the men who wanted to analyse and understand God vision with mind. Mind is always sceptical. Hence faith is incomplete. When mind tries to perceive God vision, conflict and friction appear in human relations. Hence mystic did not open themselves to everyone who approached them. They were receptive towards those who are capable of seeing soul vision. In other words a right man is required for spiritual values. In our scriptures it can be noticed that great prophets cautioned their disciples not to reveal the mystic vision to all who are not capable to perceive through the soul.

This soul vision can be made known to the mortals where love of the Supreme remains supreme, and love for lesser things like reasons, luxury, comfort, attachment, power and vain glory should not have any hold on them. Detachment has to be developed. It has a positive meaning. It is not just detachment from the worldly things. It has a positive connotation. According to Sri Rama Krishna *Vairagya* (detachment) is not merely distaste for the world, but it is an attempt to know that an earthly life cannot give solace and comfort. To Gandhi detachment means "renounce and enjoy." It is the love and light which a mortal cannot get. What is the use of this glitter if it does not put on the track of immortality. Gandhi was never close to this concept. His aim was not to structure the man with the mystic matrix. His aim was to soften the man towards his fellow men but not against the evil or a brute force. His aim was to remove the fang in man so that he cannot sting others. It is possible only through nonviolent and a right understanding of the ethos of nonviolence. Holding on to truth at any cost gives requisite patience to and follow nonviolent path. At this point Gandhi was more a powerful instrument of social engineering than a luminous light on the mortals who need light. Gandhi remained a politician and a social reformer incessantly trying for political emancipation of India and her social reconstruction. Forays into the attempt to purge the evils in the Hindu rituals and practices were way side activities on his march towards freedom and social reform. His thrust was not to get himself identified with the Supreme seeking bliss. He was busy ameliorating the conditions of the poor and to bring succour to them. To this end the means adopted were unorthodox and novel. He leaned on reason. He tested every religious saying and teaching with reason. Accordingly interpreted the Hindu scriptures. The scriptures which augmented his creed of nonviolence were grabbed and presented to the masses in a religious pack. But the idea may be essentially secular and nothing to do with the concepts like religion and God. He took ideal maxims from other religions. Interpreted in the light of nonviolence and presented to the masses as a fundamental truth. He correlated these ideas with Hinduism. But he never tried to remain a *Yogi*. Neither has love and instinct for yogihood. Gandhi's conception of yogihood revolved round regularity in life "single minded," patriotism and simplicity. At this stage the overtone of rationalist ideas in Gandhi is discernible. Gandhi never experienced any spiritual experience akin to mystic's experience. Neither he was a blind believer in religion. Nor he gained strength through religion. His strength was his faith in his masses. It solely hinged on nonviolence and *Satyagraha*.

Indian mystics always made it a point that "Divine is realisable and worth realising."[13] Otherwise lesser mortals remain at the outer fringe without being able to penetrate deeper and nearer towards the centre. The possibility of admitting the fact of soul vision brings the ordinary mortals to the start line. Unless, one attempts ceaselessly always knocking at his gate till he is unconscious, soul vision alludes him. Gandhi read much about religion. But he never tried to come on to the start line to search God. Had he been in this direction he would have been a Ramana Maharishi or a Ramakrishna Parmahansa.

Compared with a mystic, Gandhi did not see the world as a mystic sees. Mystic sees the world in a totally different light. To him the world is full of misery. Only detachment from the mundane things brings happiness and salvation is possible. Thus mystic looks at this world in a totally different light. This light changes the entire landscape. One gets detached from the calling of destiny. For this consummation, pride of knowledge and reasoning have to be shed. This was not the case with Gandhi. He was a politician among politicians and a diplomat among diplomats. He was an excellent politician and a skilful diplomat. He understood the things through mind. Approached towards the problems of the poor with heart. His faith lies in his instruments capable of transforming individual rather than in religion and faith.

Gandhi never believed in any *Sadhus* bordering on mystics. He was totally influenced by the people like Tolstoy, Ruskin and Raichandra. From Tolstoy's life three things attracted him; (1) Tolstoy did what he preached.[14] (2) His advocacy of nonviolence and[15] (3) futility of acquiring material things for comfort.[16]

Reasoning leads to the foundation of scientific spirit and method. This contributed towards material comfort. But the good for all and the luxury for all remain unfulfilled. Result is misery, squalor and poverty. All this makes the demon in man more diabolical. At this juncture the guidance of a mystic to the people becomes an imperative need. Any amount of reason does not free the man from the urge towards monstrosity. It is only spiritual values and spiritual experience makes man humane. Gandhi ceaselessly attempted to control monster under the skin of man. His aids in this regard were nonviolence and *Satyagraha*. These are the qualities of heart, not of soul. Thus his diagnosis is different from the diagnosis of a mystic to remove this malady.

Faith takes a particular course. Association with a mystic is the first stage. It gives a flick of experience to a follower from his *Guru*. The third stage is the guidance from his *Guru*. The path is littered with hidden pitfalls. Journey is arduous and perilous. But the pilgrim gets support from his *Guru*. Ultimately he has to stand firm on his legs. En route one does not get any appreciation. It is only at the final stages he will experience soul vision. All this is based on faith.

At the initial stage faith sprouts. This will develop into a colossus monolith. Ultimately this will remain unwavered. In the final stages mysticism is verifiable. The divine spark in the heart gets glow. This glow is for self enlightenment. It has no relevance to the environment outside. Hence a mystic hardly looks at his surroundings to improve the society in which he lives. He feels that his life is enough to set an example for others to remain away from evil. Best minds in the world thought about the improvement of society and had drawn a frame for the same. Their energies had been diverted towards the reconstruction of society and the individual and tried to bind the two into a just system. Gandhi had put more emphasis upon refinement of the man. Self enlightenment or pursuit of enlightenment never dominated him. He approved and appreciated qualities required for *Vairagya* and vision to look at the world with heart. Love and compassion dominated his calculations. He was never dependent upon the invisible maker of this universe.

A mystic feels that faith alone leads to enlightenment and makes one immune from misery. Intellect doubts this assertion. Hence the question that crops up is, can escapism really deliver goods? Escapism is not the hallmark of mystics. Buddha did not want to attain '*Nirvana*' till the suffering from pain and craving were removed. Similarly the Christ, embodiment of love and compassion aimed at establishing the Kingdom of God. All this indicates that man should transcend his limitations. He becomes a full man. Human ego gets sacrificed at the altar of true human being. This concept of true human being is higher than the rational humanism. The latter softens the life of the man, removes friction in human relations and social environment. But spiritual regeneration in man has a definite role to play in making the individual fit to be able to answer certain fundamental questic ıs connected with the living. These questions trouble the human mind. Like, what is the purpose of living? Where are we moving? Is there a goal? What is the meaning behind the birth and death? Many more questions like these trouble the bewildered man. Some feel that the understanding of the humanity leads to the understanding of man. Whereas a mystic says understanding of the creator leads to the understanding of the creation. It is like knowing the writer facilitates to know more of his literary piece. Science, economics, politics, sociology, psychology etc.

describe man and analyse his behaviour, whereas spiritual values make man see through himself. In the attainment of spiritual values man does not go through books, on the contrary books go through him. Gandhi was never interested in this sort of spiritual exercise. His sole concern was the improvement of ethical values.

Another important aspect in a mystic is Godliness. This separates him from the rest of humanity. Godliness makes him to be in communion with God. His spirituality gets sustenance because of his communion with God. He experiences the contact. He goes beyond the limits of God lovers. God lovers become slaves whereas a mystic while speaking in terms of spirituality blazes the path of truth. Gandhi when brought on to this format, he was in search of truth which is God. He was an all powerful *Satyagrahi*. His Godliness confines to the efficacy of his method of nonviolence. He is different from men who are God lovers and mystics whose Godliness makes them to see through themselves. Gandhi was neither a God lover as understood in common parlance nor he tried to base himself on Godliness. His mission was different and entirely novel. Not only he attracted God lovers but also atheists like Gora, agnostics like Jawaharlal Nehru and pacifists like Badshah Khan and C.F. Andrews. Further a mystic like Sivananda tried to check his ideas with him. It is a question of mysticism back tracking to politics.

Gandhi did not fit into the format of a mystic. A mystic remains in contact with the people who are on the path towards Godliness. He loves them. He thinks always about God. Talks about the love or spirituality and sacred books are in his domain. He does not desire neither money nor fame. His passion is for the Lord. He concentrates on eternal. Ephemeral has no meaning to him. A mystic always remains dead to the world, because the core of his consciousness and daily life get shifted from the mundane world. He is neither a philosopher nor a religious preacher. A mystic belongs to nowhere as he remains in perpetual contact with God. Therefore a mystic is always viewed as a bundle of idiosyncrasies, simple soul and naive. He interprets every thing in the light of the experience undergone because of his soul vision. Gandhi was never viewed by the others in this light. He interpreted events not in terms of mystic experience but in terms of politics and economics. His passion was to ameliorate the material condition of the downtrodden. He anticipated things in the light of politics and economics. His talk of religion. God, and faith has mundane values to improve human mechanism.

In the sphere outside the spiritual realm knowledge outcome of intellect takes prominence. Knowledge is mainly a product of mind. But the people who follow the path of divine aspire for the supremacy of the heart. This makes a mystic embalm over a vexed soul. He attracts the people who are capable of and want to see God in action. A mystic aspires self-knowledge. It is different from self. Gandhi though an apostle of peace and nonviolence was different from the Buddha. Gandhi's knowledge mainly confined to the knowledge that is the product of mind. He knew that he cannot apply this for knowing his self. No doubt heart rules his actions. The domination of heart in him was his conviction rather than the result of any spiritual yearning in him.

Another interesting aspect of mystic is the approaches of *Bhaktas* and *Jnana Yoga* which leads a mystic towards God. This aspect of mysticism never touched Gandhi and his meaning of religion. He told and preached to look into divinity in man. Recognition of divinity in man was more important to him. The next step in his scheme of things is to stir this divinity to make the individual an effective instrument to improve the individual and society. His love of nonviolence and search for Truth which he styled himself as his experiments with Truth, made him to devise a happy blend of *Bhakti* and *Jnana Marg*. These two are blended in right proportions. *Bhakti yoga* is visible in his approach to problem's with heart. And in the remedy he prescribed was nonviolence. By this means he tried to bring succour to the needy. *Jnana yoga* in Gandhi reflected in his experiments in Truth. He understood the play of nature, and place of the individual in it. He was dependent at the same time both on his intellect and heart simultaneously. The result was: pulls on him in different directions. He appeared contradictory. Because of this type of pull he could not become a mystic with all the trappings of a mystic present in him.

While attributing mystic qualities in Gandhi, Gandhians quote his utterances like 'inner voice',[17] and likened to mystical experience. But Gandhi never said about the content of inner voice. Further writers commented on 'inner light' in him. The inner light should be supported with inner voice to be more effective. This leads to inspiration. Inspiration makes the man blind to the environment around him. He gets immersed in soul vision. This type of inspiration was not found in Gandhi. It is because he was not following the path that leads to enlightenment. He was following a path to educate the individual to see the best in him.

Thus 'inner voice' and 'inner light' are nothing but the internal craving to be always on the right path and to exercise the goodness in man. He wrote: "My firm belief is that he reveals himself daily to every human being but we shut our ears to the still small voice we shut out eyes to the pillar of fire in front of us."[18] This statement of Gandhi has all the ingredients of theology if analysed from the Gandhian angle it will be more clear. He had not said anything about religion and God. Firstly, at the outset he had never believed in any denominational belief or religion. Secondly, his God is Truth. He was experimenting with truth till he breathed last. In this declaration he was hinting at divinity in man. He had always felt this divinity. It will grow on a nonviolent soil where prejudices do not matter. But subduing of evil in man is important. Any unethical approach or lead brings forth evil in man in the form of violence. There the sane voice of conscience which the 'inner voice' in this case has to be followed. The 'Pillar of fire' which he had hinted is the ever present brute in man. Because of the belief that his agitations when turned violent, seeing pillar of fire in front of him he had called off his movement. This statement of Gandhi has to be stripped off of the theistic coat on it. Further at no stage in his life Gandhi claimed any sainthood or prophethood.[19] He demurred even the word gospel associated to his name.[20] As a matter of fact when this word attached to his name pained him much. His entire life was devoted towards, political, social and humanitarian work.[21] His work is ethical in content and colour. On the eve of launching any political movement or deciding to undertake fast he spoke things like 'inner voice', 'inner light', God etc. only to intensify the struggle. Thus he had always tried to catch the imagination of the masses. This was never for his self salvation nor for the salvation of his followers. It was always to bring moral force and ethical guidance to his follower to move forward. At the same time this is a method of safeguarding against eruption of violence. Violence stimulates baser qualities in man. The phrase like 'inner voice' and 'inner light' or words like God and religion have specific meaning, different from the common meaning associated with them. Divinity in Gandhi cannot be denied. On the contrary he was divine totally. But it did not contribute anything towards mysticism in him. His divinity is totally different from the divinity in a mystic. The latter may remain indifferent towards the pain in others. But the former approaches them with a balm in his hand to remove the pain. He even went to the extent of helping the people not only who face pain but infinite pain to right a wrong. This was his technique to reform and to purify the individual for his emancipation politically and economically.

His mission of emancipation of man which he had experienced by putting faith in the divinity of man became the beacon light to Gandhi. This aims at both the inner voice and inner light in him. Any deviation from it is repellent to him. Always conscience guided him. Gandhi wrote: "I must not suppress the voice within, call it 'conscience', call it 'the prompting of my inner basic nature". There is something within me impelling me to cry out my agony. I have known humanity. I have studied something of psychology though I have not read many books on it. Such a man knows exactly what it is. That something in man, which never deceives me tells me now 'you have to stand against the whole world although you may have to stand alone. You have to stare the world in the face although the world may look at you with blood shot eyes. Do not fear, trust that little thing which resides in the heart. It says "forsake friends, wife, all, but testify to that for which you have lived, and for which you have to die."[22] The whole thing is clear as crystal. The energy and righteousness behind his mission always propelled him into action. At this stage that the thin edge that separates the Gandhians and the admirers of Gandhi disappears. The sceptics and agnostics even atheists associated with him in action and declared that they were not associated with him in thought. In this category of men the perception for reforming and refining man get distorted because of the dominance of struggle for freedom. The mighty current of political revolution dominated and swept the concept of restructuring man for his vitalisation. It was only in Gandhi, though he was leading the battle, the vision to uplift the man from evil never got lost. It always remained as a guide. It pushed him to choose and change symbols and slogans in his march towards freedom. This aspect tied him to the common masses. Therefore there was no pull towards mysticism. His purpose was emancipation but not enlightenment unlike a mystic.

REFERENCES

1. *The Great People of Faith Wisdom*: Readers Digest, Publication, 1984, p. 5.
2. Iravati Karve, *Yuganta* (The End of An Epoch), Sangam Books, New Delhi, 1974, p. 7.
3. John Levy, *Immediate Knowledge and Happiness*, Thorsons Publishers, London, 1970, p. 10.
4. J.H. Dave, *Immortal India*, Vol. I, Bharatiya Vidya Bhavan, Bombay, 1957.
5. M.K. Gandhi, *The Story of My Experiments with Truth*. Part II, Chapter I.
6. Dr. R.D. Ranade, *The Conception of Spiritual Life in Mahatma Gandhi and Hindu Saints*. Gujarat Vidya Sabha, Ahmedabad, 1956, p. 137.
7. *Ibid*.
8. Prof. Dr. R.D. Ranade, *The Conception of Spiritual Life in Mahatma Gandhi and Hindu Saints*, Gujarat Vidya Sabha Ahmedabad, 1956, pp. 72-75.
9. *Op. cit*., pp. 72-73.
10. *Op. cit*., pp. 74-75.
11. *Harijan*, 22 September 1940.
12. Prof. R.D. Ranade, *The Conception of Spiritual Life in Mahatma Gandhi and Hindu Saints*, p. 75.
13. Raghavan Iyer, *The Moral and Political Writings of Mahatma Gandhi*, Vol. I, Clarendon Press, Oxford, 1986, p. 186.
14. *Op. cit*., p. 113.
15. *Op. cit*., pp. 109, 113.
16. *Op cit*., pp. 107, 108.
17. *Op cit*., p. 72.
18. *Young India*, 25 May, 1921.
19. *Young India*, 11 September 1924.
20. Krishnadas, *Seven Months with Mahatma Gandhi*, Navajeevan Publishing House, Ahmedabad 1961, p. 73.
21. *Young India*, 11 September, 1924.
22. From the speech in English by Gandhi on 'Quit India' Resolution at the historic AICC Session in Bombay on 18 August 1942. Quoted in his *Search of the Supreme*, Vol. III, p. 261.

5

ATHEIST STREAK IN GANDHI

WAS Gandhi an Atheist? May be or may not. Answer was yes and no. Yes with bold indelible strokes and no with light lines. Did he believe in God ? Yes, but in truth. But not, as God is understood by the common masses. Or as understood by a *Mahant* if at all a *Mahant* understands. Or as understood by an intellectual. What was the religion of Gandhi? His religion was to bring man to a way of life where evil in him is subdued by divinity in him. Was he a mystic ? He was almost at the door step of mysticism. His purpose was different and his aim was clear. His mysticism confined to choosing appropriate religious and political symbols in his war against colonialism, exploitation and violence.

To the gullible and credulous Gandhi was a theist believing in Hinduism, drew inspiration and rejuvenation from the religion in which he was born. But to a man who sees the suffering and evaluates everything to know the truth applies a different criteria altogether to know and understand Gandhi. To men of science every discovery and invention in different fields are steps towards revelation of truth. At one stage while discussing with Gandhi the noted physicist Dr. C.V. Raman told: "If there is a God we must look for him in the universe. If he is not there. He is not there. He is not worth looking for. I am being looked upon in various quarters as an atheist but I am not. The growing discoveries in the science of astronomy and physics to me are further revelation of God. Mahatmaji's religions cannot unite. Science offers best opportunity for a complete fellowship. All men of science are brothers."[1] To this Gandhi counter questioned, "What about the converse? All who are not men of science are not brothers"?[2] C.V. Raman understood the meaning implied in these two counter questions and said: "But all can become men of science."[3]

What is the meaning of the conversation between a socially oriented seer and a scientist? The former is concerned with the common masses and their uplift from misery and squalor is important to him rather than talk of God and theism. Gandhiji did feel the necessity of emphasising that he was not an atheist but searching for truth. To him truth is well defined which he made as his aim and destination. He viewed the men as ultimate truth. The divinity in him has to be ignited. To a scientist, his revelations are just preliminary steps towards the truth. Knowledge placed the individual at the periphery of truth. He is at constant endeavour to see the core.

Gandhi found certain ethics in the religious minded scientist. He gave the example of Dr. Henry Drummon and his book "Natural in the Spiritual world." And said that similar ideas are found in the *Gita* too. The sanctity of life is the governing principle to ameliorate the conditions of man. Further there is difference between the human life and lower creation. The instinct for perpetuating the race demands the sacrifice of the individual for the sake of species. Throughout the Gandhian semantic this had become axiomatic. The aim was clear. Whether, Gandhi interpreted religion, scriptures, or politics and economics, he kept his aim and purpose clear. He had never deviated from this straight path. Though at times his statements and writings mostly issued from political pulpits seem to be contradictory. Contradiction disappears if these are put to searching examination. While speaking on contradictions in his statements arising due to contradictory declarations among various religions, Gandhi wrote: "I have no difficulty in hitting upon the truth, because I go by certain fundamental maxims. Truth is superior to everything and I reject what is in conflict with it. Similarly that which is in conflict with nonviolence should be rejected. And on matter which can be reasoned out that which conflicts must also be rejected."[4] This explains the myth behind the conflicting statements of Gandhi specially he looked more contradictory and inconsistent when he tried to tread in the realms of religion. At no stage and in no context he explained what religion is? But at every stage he took pains to explain the inner meaning of scriptures of all religions and captivated the masses. He recognised the importance of religion to push the masses on to path of revolution and struggle for freedom. But rejected religion to govern the lives of the masses. He made ethics, not religion, the beacon light for the masses to march towards his destination. He was successful. The result was, he attracted the lay and the priest as well, the intellectual, the rebel and the common man.

Gandhi kept certain fundamentals as guiding principles on his destination : He always went by these : Hence he was confident that he could reach truth; the sanctity of human and subhuman life. The result was unalloyed nonviolence. To him nonviolence is both a creed and an aim. At the same time it was his guide in all his activities. Nonviolence bears pure Gandhian hue and stamp. He practised nonviolence for a period of more than sixty years in all aspects of his struggle. He practised not only in his personal sphere, but also he brought on to the public stage and involved the masses in it. It became a creed to be pactised for political coercion against exploitations. To explain what is nonviolence is difficult. But to practise which it is an operational technique in a struggle against injustice which is intelligible and has been appreciated.

Gandhi knew that even an iota of deviation in nonviolence breeds misery and agony. The aim to remove these fails. He was considered as an idealist. But because of practice of nonviolence on a mass scale he was styled as a practical idealist.[5] He saw divinity in men. He was confident to refine the man. He felt that he could make the man to conquer the evil in him. He became an optimist. He was firm in his belief that the man is capable of developing to the highest stage possible. His optimism and his aim to remove agony and misery in the lives of people made Gandhi to practise nonviolence in all aspects of life where the unseen power i.e. sanctity of life gets momentum and assists the laws of universe. While explaining nonviolence he had drawn at times certain limits. But very often he even went to the extent of preaching the necessity and sometimes sanctity also to cross these limits. The result was that he appeared very often inconsistent contradicting his own statements. But as far as the aim was concerned it was a beacon of light beckoning him putting on the right path. Hence he became an apostle and his mission apostolic. During this voyage he explained his concept through reason, experience and faith. When he took the help of experience and faith the shades of mysticism and religion became darker and longer in his thought. For an ordinary follower to extricate

Gandhi from theology becomes difficult. Every concept of his has to be isolated, judged corelating with events and then integrated in the light of religion, politics and economics. Hence it has become a fashion on the part of those who do not penetrate deep into Gandhian thought to term Gandhian ideas on religion as liberation of theology. Some even described Gandhian ideas on religion as Gandhian theology, but not Gandhian secularism. Gandhian secularism embraces both the meanings of secularism as anti religion and as equality of religions. In other words the inner core of religion is identical with all religions.

From this the 'principle of means justifying the end' emerged. Violence cannot be removed by violence. Violence cannot wipe out violence. Violence has to be met by nonviolence. Physical force has to be opposed by soul force. Any deviation will be a hurdle on the path of progress. Option for violence hinders refinement of man. Whenever any deviation took place Gandhi experimented with Truth, which had been the sole foundation of life and remained before him giving strength to him.

Wherever and whenever ideas appeared to strengthen his conviction on nonviolence Gandhi borrowed from the East as well as the West.[6] What was important to him was human activity and achievement. The high voltage of ideas in religion as against the forces that negated the philosophy beyond religion were the source of inspiration to probe into the heart of man for his infinite capacity towards development. He felt that human achievement in the domain of culture is the product of heart and soul of the individual. It gives continuity. Progress depends upon continuity and change as well with least friction. Nonviolence forms the oily film between the surfaces of continuity and change. Nonviolence therefore is not an empty slogan. It has specific role to play in the onward movement of the individual.

Change and continuity signifies the momentum of life. In other words it is human activity. There is immense possibility of violence in this activity because of the acquisitive nature of man. This can be countered only by nonviolence. Religion never speaks about nonviolence because of its sectarian interest. Philosophy on the other hand aims at improvement of human life pushing the man to accept truth the sanctity of life. Human peace and happiness are possible when this is accepted. Aims of philosophy and religion in seeking improvement of human life are not congruent. At no stage Gandhi took the help of religion and its practice for human happiness and peace. In this context his religion was nonviolence and his God was Truth. Truth was God. The central meaning of his philosophy was human activity for continuity and change without friction. He upheld not only this sanctity of human life but also subhuman life as well.

Gandhi always viewed that the individual is capable of self-development. He always felt that the virtues which Gandhiji called divinity in man can be cultivated even in the wicked where the brute dominates over humanism. This reveals invisible insulation over the sanctity of human life. These virtues when confront with evil in man, Truth appears more vividly than any other aspect in human activity. Ultimately the moral force in human heart prevails. To this moral force in man, Gandhi called ethical religion. This makes it possible for everyone to see the 'Kingdom of God' within. At the twilight zone of this 'Kingdom' the instinct of sacrifice for the sake of others gets ignited releasing the greatest energy in man unconceived. The fusion of sacrifice and service for and to man elevates divinity in man. Consequently unlimited potential for self development is visible. In saying this Gandhi had said nothing new, yet emphasized the fact, as available in this world.

Thus the source of moral force in man initiates the process to eliminate the brute in man. Human evolution takes place. The more the brute in man is eliminated the more the creed of nonviolence is practised. He emphasised this wherever opportunity arose. Gandhi had tried and succeeded to interpret scriptures and religion to uphold nonviolence. He took the help of religion to sanctify his principle. Educated the masses about nonviolence and its efficacy through the medium of theology. He took the help of theology because his audience were illiterate and seeped in religion and superstition. He wanted an acceptable medium and found it in religion. He did not believe in any denominational religion, nor practised, nor asked to follow a particular religion. His slogan to Hindus was to become a better Hindu, to Muslims a better Muslim and to Christians a better Christian. He thus wanted to steel the moral fibre in man to make him an effective instrument in the service of humanity.

Gandhi's entire activity was based on nonviolence. When Gandhi was being dragged into political ideology it was an attempt to identify

Gandhi with anarchists and radicals of various hue and creed. But he emphatically denied that he was not associated with any of these ideologies or ideologues. His ideology was nonviolence. When his creed of nonviolence compelled him to associate with radicals and anarchists[7] and to all those who believe in nonviolence he looked like an anarchist or a radical. This association was a product of his faith in him to be capable of weaning away the masses from the path of violence. Gandhi wrote: "My path is clear. Any attempt to use me for violent purposes is bound to fail. I have no secret methods. I know no diplomacy save that of truth. I have no weapon but nonviolence. . . . I do not believe in short violent ends to success. I am an uncompromising opponent of violent methods even to serve the noblest of causes. There is, therefore, really no meeting ground between the school of violence and myself. But my creed of nonviolence not only does not preclude, but compels me even to associate with anarchists and all those who believe in violence. But, yet, association is always with the sole object of weaning them from what appears to me to be their error. For experience convinces me that permanent good can never be the outcome of untruth and violence".[8]

Gandhi's nonviolence was his religion and his truth was his God. He believed in nonviolence and its efficacy in bringing about desired results in all human activities where coercion can be eliminated. These were his ideals and the very "breath of his life"[9] Gandhi successfully applied this creed of nonviolence against colonialism. And his symbols that he had chosen for various battles in his war against colonialism were intelligible to the common mass and inspired them. He was forthright to accept the want of efficacy of nonviolence in the face of communal violence and in the wars between the nations. His explanation to the first was, that nonviolence as a principle of passive resistance was practised. Throughout the period that followed Gandhi's advent in national politics nonviolence practised was not nonviolence but passive resistance of the weak. It was suppressed energy. Hence when controls were lifted outcome of energy resulted in communal violence and internecine war.[10] The belief in nonviolence as a weapon of the strong was not there. Hence, its application in wars between nations is not possible.[11] Nonviolence if it is effective, should be the weapon of the strong. Accordingly nonviolence should not be identified with passive resistance. At the stage of practising to wield nonviolence as an effective weapon it requires "proper training and proper generalship."[12]

Gandhi never lost faith in nonviolence as a creed or his religion to know the truth as his God. These two guided him to look into the scriptures and religious lore of every religion. He delved deep into these. Fathomed the depths. Brought the gems out of the bottom. His slogan, therefore, was that before one styles himself a Hindu he should search himself whether he can adorn the gems he had in his own religion. Similar advice he had given to the Christians, the Muslims and others. Before a Hindu calls himself a Hindu he should try to become a better Hindu. Similarly he told the Christians before calling themselves as christians they should strive to become better Christians. Similarly he advised the Muslims before labelling themselves as Muslims they should struggle to become better Muslims. Keeping this in view Gandhi did not lose a single opportunity to examine religious maxims and sayings in the light of the principle of nonviolence, and thus tried to aim at truth.

Since Gandhi believed and followed the teachings of the *Gita* and the *Sermon on the Mount*, how was it that he was secular but not theistic ? It is a genuine doubt yet valid. His entire interpretation of the *Gita* bears the testimony of his theme : the improvement of man to see himself. This theme dominated his interpretation of the *Gita*. It has become axiomatic with him. Any scripture he found suitable he interpreted accordingly. He made the *Gita* his mother[13] to guide him through the trials and temptation of life. He mastered seven hundred verses. He called the "*Gita* the essence of all the *Sastras* and the *Upanishads*."[14] He understood the meaning and interpreted it to support his theme. He wrote: "Today *Gita* is not only my *Bible* and *Koran*; it is more than that, it is my mother. I lost my mother early who gave me birth long ago; but this eternal mother has completely filled her place by my side ever since. She has never changed, she has never failed me when I am in difficulty or distress. I seek refuge in her."[15] With this devotion Gandhi approached the *Gita* to interpret things whenever he was confused at the conflicting opinions of the learned *Pundits* of Hinduism. Interpretations of these *Pundits* never created gospels in him. He was guided by his aim of searching truth and practising nonviolence.

Gandhi was aware of the fact that the *Gita* is not a treatise on nonviolence nor was it written to denounce war. Hinduism as has been practised today does not condemn war as Gandhi did.[16] What Gandhi had done was, that he gave a novel yet logical and natural interpretation to the *Gita* and the spirit of Hinduism in it.[17] Hinduism is ever evolving. It has no single book like *Bible* or *Koran* as the Christians and the Muslims are having. *Karma*, *Sanyasa* and *Yagna* acquired new meaning. It gave new life and vigour to Hinduism. This constant evolution to the meaning attached to the *Gita*, envigorated not only the original meaning but the secular concepts evolved from it. This made the *Gita* a live scripture to be followed for sustenance and vigour.

The two books, the *Ramayana* and the *Mahabharata*, which every Hindu regards as his guide, to Gandhi these two books deal with the eternal duel that goes on between the forces of darkness and light.[18] In this light Gandhi looked at the *Gita* and interpreted it to reform the individual.

The *Gita* is a source of attraction both to the lay and the intellectual. One would find encyclopaedic learning in Tilak's *Gita Rahasya.* Similar is the case with the interpretation of the *Gita* by great people like Aurobindo Ghosh and others. Gandhi wanted to make the *Gita* an easy book to read and to comprehend his interpretation to a lay reader. He wrote: "If you find all the eighteen chapters too difficult to negotiate make a careful study of the first three chapters only. They will give you in a nutshell what is propounded in greater detail and from different angles in the remaining fifteen chapters. Even these three chapters can be further epitomised in a few verses that can be selected from these chapters. Add to this the fact that at three distinct places the *Gita* goes even further and exhorts us to leave all 'isms' and take refuge in the Lord alone, and it will be seen how baseless is the charge that the message of the *Gita* is too subtle or complicated to lay minds to understand. The *Gita* is the universal mother. She turns away nobody. Her door is wide open to any one who knocks. A true votary of the *Gita* does not know what disappointment is. He ever dwells in perennial joy and peace that passeth understanding. But that peace and joy come not to the sceptic or to him who is proud of his intellect and learning. It is reserved only for the humble in spirit who brings to her worship a fullness of faith and an undivided singleness of mind. There never was a man who worshipped her in that spirit and went back disappointed."[19] At the outset two aspects Gandhi emphasised: "taking refuge in the Lord and humility. The first relates to the divinity in man. The second i.e. humility tempers the individual to accept self-realization and selflessness as goals of life. These two dominate Gandhian theism and form the essence of his religion. Keeping these two in views Gandhi made the *Gita* as a sort of reference book for his guidance. He called the *Gita* as his "spiritual dictionary."[20] It has a universal appeal free from dogma and sectarianism. It is not an abstruse book. Gandhi felt that a man of ordinary intelligence does not find it difficult to follow the message in the *Gita*.

What message did the *Gita* convey according to Gandhi? A difficult question to answer. Critics pointed out that to interpret the *Gita* in support of his creed of *Ahimsa* was not justified. At the first opportunity Gandhi studied the *Gita* in Gujarati translation. It whetted his appetite for more.[21] He read several works on the *Gita*. And tried to interpret the message in it to suit his scheme of things.

After a thorough assimilation Gandhi called the *Gita* his "spiritual reference book".[22] and interpreted the *Gita* in the light of his *Ahimsa* and his search for truth. He felt that the central theme of the *Gita* is selfrealisation and selflessness. The former urges man to look into self. That is searching divinity in self. Once the divinity is located man will be on the improvement trail. Wisdom and virtue add substance to knowledge and intelligence. At this stage virtue instead of intelligence guides. The path will be blazed with wisdom, not knowledge. No longer will there be vacillation in mind between apocalyptic fears and mystical yearnings. Ambition gets curbed. The evil in man can be eliminated. Civilization can remain stable. There will not be any wage for sin, since sin does not guide. Wisdom and virtue are beacon lights to reach destination.

Closely following self realisation is selflessness. It comes on to surface once the principle of 'renunciation of fruits of action'[23] the corner stone of the *Gita* becomes the guiding principle in one's own action. Gandhi called it a 'matchless remedy.'[24] He wrote, "This is the centre round which devotion, knowledge and the rest revolve like planets."[25] Man remains active perpetually. To live in activity is essential. All activity is purposive and motivated with self. As long as selfishness in the form of fruits for action remains, the body where God dwells or divinity resides will be tainted with sin. Divinity cannot shine in man as long as man remains selfish. Man becomes a victim of his sins. Evil in him dominates. The remedy is desireless action.

Desireless or renunciation does not dawn for mere awareness or its importance. There should be devotion to achieve this. And devotion is nothing but a quality in a sage.[26] The qualities of a sage constitute divinity in man. At this stage Gandhi wanted that the heart should rule the mind. In this context Gandhi did not place much importance to faith which is the fulcrum of religion.

Further elaborating the principle of knowledge and devotion to man Gandhi enunciated his principle of means justifying the end not *vice versa*.[27] Knowledge and devotion are not media of exchange to get certain qualities in man. The possession of these is essential. These two are required for improvement. They are absolute. Any limitation hinders the individual in his endeavour towards self realisation.

Action is the second stage from knowledge and devotion. At this stage Gandhi was more a social reformer and a revolutionary. From the realms of spirituality he descends on to activity on mundane things. To him, activity is essential. Life gets meaning and purpose through activity. No activity however menial and ordinary or common practice is unimportant. Every action whose purpose is to maintain life and body has a definite place in society. One has to earn his bread. One has to live. A *Bhakta* leaves his rosary only for drinking and eating etc. and if he refuses to grind corn or nursing patient is not a *Bhakta*. Thus Gandhi gave more importance to socially useful work, rather than prayer and meditation. These have their own place in the Gandhian scheme of things. Yet these are not essential to bring succour to the people. Emphasising this point Gandhi further pointed out that Janaka the legendary king in *Ramayana* who was a wise sage could attain salvation through action only.

Thus activity is important for sustenance of our society. Ceasing work means inactivity. This leads to fall of society. It is action that binds one another. Action includes both mental and physical action. In other words it is detachment from the fruits of a piece of work.

Desire for reward for work has to be renounced. He who does not work falls to perish. He who does not desire reward rises above. This does not mean ignorance of the result of action. It means one should be aware of the result and get engrossed towards the fulfilment of the task renouncing fruits of action.

Renunciation of reward means renunciation in hankering advantage. On the other hand the thought of acquiring reward stands to hinder the spontaneity performance of one's duties. This want of spontaneity makes one to fix his aim at reward. If the desire is not fulfilled, he becomes impatient leading to anger. He will remain vacillating and bids farewell to all scruples. The result will be that he will opt for the principle 'end justifying the means'. In other words evil overtakes divinity in man. Restructuring man to improve society does not take place. Creed of nonviolence gets stunted. The sanctity of life is discounted.

There is nothing religion in this. Religion aims at salvation. It is emancipation of man from evil within. In activities, of course socially useful other than religion worldly pursuits dominate. In reality there is no distinction or line of demarcation between these two viz. salvation and worldly pursuits. In day-to-day life the acts performed with a motive are taboo. According to Gandhi these acts are murder, lying, dissoluteness and the like. These are sinful and therefore taboo. The moment man becomes simple and avoids materialism his activities remain socially useful. There will not be any taboo on these. Spontaneity to perform one's duty eliminates craving for reward. This will lead to selflessness in man.

Selflessness leads to truth and *Ahimsa*. In the absence of desire for gain in any activity temptation for untruth and *Ahimsa* is removed. At the back of untruth and violence temptation stalks. The *Gita* was written to remove temptation behind every activity. Consequently the motivation for *Ahimsa* increases and ultimately truth will be established. The machanics of Gandhian thought which emphasizes truth speaks of divinity in man.

Certain concepts like *Sanyasa* and sacrifice in the *Gita* were reinterpreted by Gandhi in relation to his philosophy of nonviolence and truth. Sacrifice in the context of the *Gita* means 'body labour for service.' The third and the fourth chapters of the *Gita* should be read in conjunction. The concept *sanyasa* does not mean cessation of all activity. It is all work yet no work. It is like a placid confluence of two mighty rivers; activity and meditation. Activity is to improve society and meditation to drive out evil in self and uncover divinity. He looked at the *Gita* through his creed *Ahimsa*. Gandhi wrote: ". . . after 40 years unremitting endeavour fully to enforce the teaching of the *Gita* in my own life. I have, in all humility felt that perfect renunciation is impossible without perfect observance of *Ahimsa* in every shape and form."[28] In his scheme of things neither the *Gita* nor the book of any other religion was important before his creed of *Ahimsa*. He viewed and interpreted every word of every scripture keeping *Ahimsa* in view. To him man is the ultimate measure of all things. A fully evil subdued man was the ideal before Gandhi.

After interpreting the main theme of the *Gita* Gandhi described the *Gita* as a "reasoned moral code" satisfying both the intellect and the heart. It is philosophical and at the same time devotional. If the principle of *Ahimsa* followed, it becomes a living creed protecting the sanctity of life where truth resides. This will lead to desired evolution of society and man for perfection. To Gandhi ritual and rites are not at all necessary. On the contrary religion and scripture should lure the individual not to float on religion with the help of ritual, rite and priest but to dive deep to pick the pearl, and the gem to strength the ethical fibre in man. To this extent Gandhi wanted religion. But the domination of religion over the individual was never preferred. The precepts and practices of religion had been intelligently used and cultivated to refine the man. It is the essence of Gandhi's ideas on religion. Gandhi wrote: "I believe that all the great religions of the world are true more or less. I say 'more or less' because I believe that everything that human hand touches by reason of the very fact that human beings are imperfect, becomes imperfect. Perfection is the exclusive attribute of God and it is indescribable and untranslatable. I do believe that it is possible for every human being to become perfect even as God is perfect. It is necessary for us all to aspire after perfection, but when that blessed state is attained, it becomes indescribable, indefinable. And I therefore admit, in all humility, that even the *Veda*, the *Koran*, and the *Bible* are the imperfect word of God, and imperfect being that we are swayed to and fro by a multitude of passions, it is impossible for us even to understand the word of God in its fullness. . . ."[29] After discarding the ritual and ceremony associated with religion Gandhi went a step further to doubt the perfection of scripture and gospel. They represent the imperfection of their originators. Exhorting to become perfect as God means, the divinity in man should come out conquering evil. Only then self realisation and selflessness are possible.

To emphasise imperfection of the book Gandhi wrote: "But I must not be misunderstood. I do not hold that everything ancient is good because it is ancient. I do not advocate surrender of God given reasoning faculty in the face of ancient tradition. Any tradition, however ancient if inconsistent with morality is fit to be banished from the land."[30] He wrote like this to condemn the abominable practice of untouchability. What did Gandhi mean, when he said that no book of religion is perfect and everything has to be in conformity with ethics and reasoning faculty. The gift of God has to be exercised to test gospel and scripture. Gandhi was clear of his aim and purpose of interpreting the book intelligible to the learned and the lay. The result was that the people seeped in religion like Vinoba Bhave, Kaka Kelkar, Mahadev Desai and Kishori Lal Mashuriwala were attracted to him. Intellectuals like Acharya Kripalani, Acharya Narendra Dev and others came near to him. An agnoistic like Jawaharlal Nehru was close to him. An atheist like Gora saw something great in Gandhi and that attracted to him. To the masses he was a *Mahatma*—a noble soul.

After interpreting the core of the *Gita*, Gandhi has gone to various aspects of this 'celestial song'. He compared the entire battle field Kurukshetra with the everpresent duel between divinity and evil in the heart.[31] Kurukshetra is always looked upon as *Dharmakshetra*. So is the heart of the man. It is a field of reghteousness. Most of the time the battle in the heart is between 'mine' and 'thine'. In other words between the irrepressible forces of selfishness and selflessness. The *Gita* always tells us to give up our likes and dislikes. This is the main teaching of the *Gita*. Similarly in all other religions it is found to those who want to see into himself. As long as this aspect which Gandhi emphasised in religion, was found, religion was not an anathema, but an effective instrument to refine man.

The entire theme of Gandhian theology is how to improve man? How to bring man on to the road of perfection? What inputs have to be created in man to restructure him? Taking the analogy from the *Gita*, Gandhi always wanted to control the senses through which pleasure and pain are felt. Wise try to withdraw from sense objects. In an average individual sense objects always dominate senses. Only when he tries to attack these sense objects he will be on the path of righteousness. This is the real battle according to Gandhi. Some people resort to fasting and mortification of flesh as instruments against sense object. But these have very limited value. It is only when man turns inward to see himself or divinity in man he can control himself. The sense objects have little effect upon him. But if on the other hand when sense objects dominate him desire arises. Very often, owing to nonfulfilment of desires makes one angry. Anger drives him mad losing all sense of proportion. This will lead to loss of memory. He thus comes to dead end of ignobility. Only when he gets control of sense objects he becomes stable minded. This will make him to see things clear. He is free from pride and selfishness. He becomes altogether a different man, and finds peace. Only thus divinity in him gets ignited.

After interpreting the core of the third chapter in the *Gita*, Gandhi wrote: "I call this chapter key to an understanding of the *Gita*, and the gist of it is that life is given to us for service and not for enjoyment. We have therefore to impart a sacrificial character to our lives. Intellectual assent to this proposition is only the first step, but such assent and conduct in terms of that assent are bound to rid our heart of its impurities in course of time. But what is real service? In order to obtain the right answer to this question, restraint of the senses is essential, as it gives us a clearer and a clearer vision of God of Truth. Service rendered with selfish motives ceases to be sacrifice. Hence the urgent need is for the spirit of detachment. When this is understood, all manner of controversies lose their meaning for us. Did Krishna really ask Arjuna to kill his relatives ? Could such killing ever be a part of one's duty ? Questions like these are set at rest for ever. When detachment governs our actions, even the weapon raised in order to strike an enemy falls down out of our hand. But mere pretence of detachment serves no useful purpose. If only we preserve in our effort, detachment may come to us, perhaps the very first day, or may be only after a thousand years. We must not worry over the time this takes, for the effort carries within itself the seeds of success. And we must however be on guard and make sure that it is genuine effort, and that there is no self deception. And this is certainly possible for us all."[32] Thus Gandhi had faith in man and the divinity in his heart. This divinity gets glow only when deception and selfishness get discouraged. It has to be cultivated laboriously leading to salvation of man.

To augment his line of thinking and to bring desired effect on man, Gandhi pleaded for *Vratas*, observance of *Brahmacharya* and the like. He wanted to practise the inputs to get the divinity in man blaze. Man is limited. The potential of divinity in man is limitless. The momentum of life gets much sanctified and fully protected only when self-realisation and selflessness became a part of man's activity. This gets creed of nonviolence strengthened, and thus propels man nearer to Truth. The sixth chapter of the *Gita* reinforces those methods which bring man nearer to Truth through nonviolence. These are *Vratas, Brahmacharya, Pranayam and Asanas*. While interpreting the fourth chapter of the *Gita*, Gandhi wrote : "A man can be saved or lost by himself alone. Therefore he becomes his own friend or his own enmy as the case may be. To one who has subdued his mind, his soul is a friend, while the soul is an enemy for him who has failed to achieve self control. The test for self control is that heat and cold, pleasure and pain, honour and dishonour do not disturb one's inner serenity. He is a *yogi* who is a man of knowledge as well as experience, who is unwavering and master of his senses and to whom gold, stone and earth all seem alike. He regards with an equal eye friend and foe, sinner and saint. With a view to attain this state a man should stabilise his mind, divert it of all sensual desires and meditate in solitude on the Supreme soul. It is not enough to practise *yogic asans* etc. In order to achieve evenness of temper, one must scrupulously keep the major observances such as *Brahmacharya* and the like. A man who thus takes his place on a firm seat keeps observances and concentrates his mind on God enters perfect peace."[33] After achieving equanimity Gandhi asked to embark on action which propels man to forward movement.

As the entire interpretation of the *Gita* revolved round action without hankering for fruit and detachment, the entire interpretation of Christianity revolved round love and compassion. As long as there is love and compassion the idea of retaliation never occurs.

Hence Gandhi wrote: "that Christianity has yet to be lived unless one says that where there is boundless love and no idea of retaliation whatsoever, it is Christianity that lives."[34] With this principle of love Gandhi looked at every movement and ism. He criticised these. But he loved the man the unit of measurement in all types of society.

Old Testament did not inspire Gandhi. He was profoundly impressed by the *New Testament.* It presented as a symbol of kingdom of God in individual and social aspects. In the *Sermon on the Mount* he found passive resistance. Later on he developed this principle into a weapon of the strong. "Gandhi's understanding and practice of the cross brought out fresh aspects of Jesus' life and character which the West had not so clearly perceived."[35] He interpreted tenets of Christianity and related these to his ideas of nonviolence and truth as was the case of his interpretations of Hinduism. To him nonviolence is not only negation of violence but also love and charity.

In a similar tone Gandhi spoke about other religions besides Christianity and Hinduism. His ideas on other religions coincide with his secular ideas which he had held to improve the individual as well as society in which he lives. From the individual side Gandhi wanted incessant toil in the service of humanity and country. Selflessness has to temper this service. On the social side Gandhi visualised an ideal society where justice is done 'unto the last' and in which institutions aim at to get the best out of man. The entire Gandhian thought in the realm of religion and secular thought as well revolves round the establishment of a just society. Social friction is negated by the creed of nonviolence. Any other creed in the attempt of removing social friction exploits man. Misery and death stalk the man. History is the witness of this phenomenon.

In waging war against injustice and colonialism, Gandhi adopted his techniques of *Satyagraha*. He did not invoke religion nor God in any conceivable form. *Satyagraha* when it was taking shape in South Africa in Natal in the year 1906, his entire concept of this technique based on two premises: first "one should not despise any man however insignificant looking he may be, secondly no matter how timid a man is, he is capable of loftiest heroism when he is put to test."[36] Further from the beginning Gandhi was convinced in the invincibility of man if the divinity in him is aroused. His divinity lies in his qualities like truthfulness, patience, tolerance, firmness, presence of mind, courage and commonsense.[37] He did not pay much importance to knowledge and learning.

From this premise, with absolute faith in man Gandhi launched *Satyagraha* against Black ordinance in 1906. To Gandhi *Satyagraha* means 'insistence of truth'. Initially he did not know what name to be given to his movement. One Shri Mangal Gandhi suggested the word '*Sodagraha*' in response to the advertisement in 'Indian opinion'. *Sodagraha* means 'firmness in good cause'. Gandhi liked the word. But he felt that it did not "fully represent the whole idea, which he wished to connote. Therefore Gandhi suggested it as '*satyagraha*'. "Truth (*Satya*) implies love, firmness (*Graha*) engenders and therefore serves as a force synonym for force." Further Gandhi wrote : "I, thus began to call the Indian movement '*Satyagraha*' that is to say the force which is born of Truth and love or nonviolence and gave up the use of phrase 'passive resistance' ". . . .[38]

Passive resistance techniques were evolved after getting inspired by the Sermon on the Mount. This mode of resistance was always considered as a weapon of the weak. This phrase was first used in England. No one knew by whom. Whenever there was any obnoxious piece of legislation was passed, the people who were affected resisted peacefully. Nonconformist resistance against Education Act under the leadership of Dr. Clifford was an example of passive resistance. Similar was the case with the movement of the English women for franchise. Gandhi had cited these examples why passive resistance was considered as a weapon of the weak.

Gandhi termed *Satyagraha* as soul force. It means holding on to truth and believing in nonviolence. There is no place for brute force in the scheme of '*Satyagraha*' the spearhead of the Indian independence movement. A *Satyagrahi* never uses force even when he suffered badly, and when he is in a position to use force effectively. Gandhi wrote: "*Satyagraha* is a soul force pure and simple, and whenever and to whatever extent there is room for the use of arms or physical force or brute force, there and to that extent is there so much less possibility for soul force. These are purely antagonistic forces in my view, and I had full realisation of this antagonism at the time of the advent of *Satyagraha*."[39] There is a clear distinction between the passive resistance and '*Satyagraha*'. Gandhi believed that the difference between the two is fundamental. *Satyagraha* indicates the inner strength of the man to resist evil. Passive resistance is the weapon of the weak, while *Satyagraha* springs from the illimitable strength of man. This idea nourishes the growth of *Satyagrahi* from strength to strength. The entire movement becomes effective.

Further elaborating the distinction between the techniques of passive resistance and *Satyagraha* Gandhi saw want of love in the former, while in the latter there was not only no place for hatred, but it is a positive breach of its ruling principle. Explaining the difference between the two Gandhi wrote: "If we are *Satyagrahis* and offer *Satyagraha* believing ourselves to be strong two clear consequences result from it. Fostering the idea of strength, we grow stronger and stronger every day. With the increase in our strength, our *Satyagraha* too becomes more effective and we would never be looking about for an opportunity to give it up. Again, while, there is no scope for love in passive resistance, on the other hand not only has hatred no place in *Satyagraha* but is a positive breach of its ruling principle. While in passive resistance there is a scope for the use of arms when a suitable occasion arrives, in *Satyagraha* physical force is forbidden even in the most favourable circumstances. Passive resistance is often looked as a proposition for the use of force while *Satyagraha* can never be utilised as such. Passive resistance may be offered side by side with the use of arms. *Satyagraha* and brute force, being each negation of the other, can never go together. *Satyagraha* may be offered to one's nearest and dearest. Passive resistance can never be offered to them unless of course they have ceased to be dear and become an object of hatred to us. In passive resistance there is always present an idea of harassing the other party and there is a simultaneous readiness to undergo any hardship entailed upon us by such activity. While in *Satyagraha* there is not the remotest idea of injuring the opponent. *Satyagraha* postulates the conquest of the adversary by suffering in one's own person."[40]

After explaining the distinction between the two Gandhi interpreted the passive resistance offered by the early Christians as *Satyagraha*. Jesus who had been admired as the "prince of passive resistance." in terms of Gandhi was an indomitable *Satyagrahi* where love and truth merge at one point. This interpretation of the early Christian resistance to evil smacks of no religion, no ritual, and no

God. In this resistance the spirit of unlimited sacrifice, pure love and radiant truth were ever present. Gandhi again introduced a secular concept to his masses with a theistic medium. And declared that love and truth made Jesus the prince of *Satyagraha*.

While explaining the concept of *Satyagraha,* Gandhi emphasised those qualities in man which make him see divinity in himself. And further pointed out that these qualities are essential to perfect the technique of *Satyagraha*. Fearlessness in a different context had been pointed out as essential to launch *Satyagraha*. In the context of *Satyagraha* it was emphasised to bring out different qualities in man. A *Satyagrahi* leaves fear. He remains totally a fearless man. He does not doubt nor is he afraid of his opponent even if the opponent plays fault with him. Gandhi wrote: "A *Satyagrahi* bids good bye to fear. He is therefore never afraid of trusting the opponent. Even if the opponent plays him false twenty times the *Satyagrahi* is ready to trust him for the twenty first time for an implicit trust in human nature is the very essence of his creed."[41] Thus a *Satyagrahi* wants to oppose his opponent with love. It requires infinite patience and ability to suffer.

Success does not lie in the outcome of the battle at the end. But success is inherent in *Satyagraha* itself. This makes *Satyagrahi* to hold on to his cause even in the face of untold suffering or even at the point of death. "The very nature of *Satyagraha* is such that the fruit of the movement is contained in the movement itself. *Satyagraha* is based on self help, self sacrifice and faith in God."[42] It is divinity in man. Further Gandhi wrote: "As a *Satyagrahi* I hold to the faith, that all activity pursued with a pure heart is bound to bear fruit, whether or not such fruit, is visible to us. And last but not the least I have tried to show that all truthful movements spontaneously attract to themselves all manner of pure and disinterested help."[43] Gandhi explained this citing the example of the co-operation and support he got from his European friends to his *Satyagraha* movement in Transval against Black Ordinance.

The entire ideal of *Satyagraha* is based on the character of *Satyagrahi*. His character is his capital.[44] This character emerges on the qualities like fearlessness, love, self sacrifice and self realisation. Because of these qualities ability to suffer to any length and infinite patience develop in man. The result will be the weak become strong.

The divinity in man becomes dynamite to blast the evil in his opponent and to get love and affection.

The principles of nonviolence and truth lead to the technique of *Satyagraha*. No doubt *Satygraha* was a forceful weapon wielded by Gandhi against violence, colonialism and exploitation. *Satyagraha* leads to a society of *Sarvodaya* where nonviolence, freedom and love prevail not only in full but in abundance. Had Gandhi spoken anything on *Satyagraha* leading to *Sarvodaya*, the theistic content could have been traced in his thought. But this was not so. Is the movement for establishing *Sarvodaya* society a secular movement or a religious movement ? Is there any religious content in *Sarvodaya* ? Or is it purely a secular ?

These questions, when seek answers will reveal the nature, content and texture of society which Gandhi had in mind. Religion did not creep into *Sarvodaya* nor *Satyagraha*. Man the ultimate measuring unit in all social sciences remains the pivot of social structure. The liberal traditions seek freedom, growth and happiness of man. In the context of *Sarvodaya* as welfare of all at no stage touches even the periphery of religion. Entire *Sarvodaya* format is a sociopolitical and economic scheme to ensure freedom, growth and happiness. At this stage, mistakenly, students of political thought trace utilitarian streak in Gandhian thought. The utilitarian design in Gandhian thought is the result of the imagination of students of political thought. His *Sarvodaya* welfare of all hinges on moral growth in man where the weak is not exploited by the strong for selfish ends. The former is helped and assisted with love to strengthen the divinity in the latter. Man is infinite in his capability to change his environment to sooth himself. Moreover Gandhi preached against materialism to remove selfishness. Utilitarian principle though a lofty one is based on selfishness. The more it is emphasised the more impetus is given to selfishness.

In *Sarvodaya* concept every aspect of man has got enmeshed with the other. The entire notion of divinity is the basis of this alchemy of mundane aspects in *Sarvodaya*. What does *Sarvodaya* mean from a political angle ? The meaning of *Swaraj* in the context of *Sarvodaya* was the liberation of India from the clutches of the British imperialism. And thus to make India capable of controlling herself. Extending this analogy Gandhi viewed that the individual should have freedom to control himself. It means the self-control of the individual.[45] Self-control leads to strengthen moral fibre in man. Individual is the medium to know the state and society. It is the restrained and self-controlled individual contributes maximum to remove friction between individuals, institutions and between individual and institutions. Gandhi wrote: "I value individual freedom but you must not forget that man is essentially a social being. He has risen to this status by learning to adjust his individualism to the requirements of social progress. Unrestricted individualism is the law of the beast, of the jungle. We have to learn to strike the mean between individual freedom and social restraint. Willing submission to social restraint for the sake of the wellbeing of the whole society enriches both the individual and society of which one is a member."[46] He had not given importance to the dictates of society asking the individual to obey these inplicitly on the contrary he placed importance on the individual pleading for selflessness and self realisation. When the people near him identified *Sarvodaya* with democracy missed the wood for tree. The significance of *Sarvodaya* could not be grasped. Emphasis was on democracy as secular concept. While others who had attached more significance to *Sarvodaya* concept vis-a-vis democracy added religion and caused euphoric ecstasy. They thought that *Sarvodaya* can be ushered in with religion as propellent. *Sarvodaya* in society is a simple concept devoting the improvement of man for an ideal society where man is incapable to exploit others. The growth of man takes place not through violent means form one stage to the other but through nonviolence.

Further elaborating *Sarvodaya* concept Gandhi held the view that a handful of people should not thrust power on the rest at the bottom. At the bottom each individual should shape himself capable of softening the political power.[47] The former should liberate the individual towards the selflessness and self realisation.

While touching the frontiers of economics Gandhi spoke of two main things viz. trusteeship and bread labour. Besides these two he spoke on every conceivable aspect of economics. Trusteeship idea takes out the power in the hands of the few rich. And the concept of bread labour provides full employment. In Gandhian context trusteeship involves mere possession of even a single grain or a stick more than what is necessary amounts to theft. Hence the rich should be the trustee of their surplus property for the sake of the poor and the weak.[48] Because everything available on earth belongs to everyone and enough for everyone.[49] Stocking and accumulation of wealth means robbing from the mouth of the weak, who has every right to live on this earth.

The trusteeship concept aims at the following[50]:

(a) A means to transform the existing society into an egalitarian society, through non-violence.
(b) Non-recognition of right to private property the only source of present day conflict and chaos.
(c) Legislative regulation over ownership and use of wealth is possible.
(d) State regulated trusteeship makes the individual impossible to hold wealth for selfish ends.
(e) Maximum income limits and minimum wage limits can be fixed.
(f) Social necessity dictates the mode of production.

The second important economic concept in the context of *Sarvodaya* is bread labour. Bread labour points out that one has to put in work to earn his own bread. He has to earn his bread with his labour. These ideas Gandhi got from Ruskin's 'Unto the Last'. A Russian writer T.M. Bondaref also stressed the importance of labour to earn one's bread. Tolstoy pleaded for this principle and made aware of this. What is the significance of it ? It aims at making man to work. No type of activity is superior to, the other. This explains importance and necessity of working with own hands. It speaks of the necessity of self reliance. All these put emphasis on employment. At no stage religion and ritual appeared in Gandhi's calculations of trusteeship and bread labour. These two aim at the removal of exploitation and making man self sufficient.

The symbols Gandhi adopted in war against colonialism were political and economic in nature than religious. His programme of *Khadi* was one of these symbols. Economic and political implications were immense. Bharatan Kumarappa a Gandhian economist wrote: "He (Gandhi) realised of course, that by making us economically independent, *Khadi* would help hastening the achievement of political freedom. The significance is not merely political. His symbols have much deeper and more permanent meaning. These have a bearing on the entire life of the people whom he was leading.

Thus for instance, Gandhi wanted our people by hand spinning to shake off inertia and a feeling of helplessness, and to learn to rely on themselves. Mill production of cloth could not secure this as, in the first place, mills could employ only a small fraction of the people, and in the second place, in mill production the employee could not be self reliant as he was dependent on the employer for wages, raw materials and machinery. It was *Khadi* alone which could teach our village population to depend on their own efforts to improve their lot and thus to learn their first lesson in real independence. *Khadi*, therefore, had for Gandhi not merely an economic significance, but also great cultural and psychological value. It was meant to put new life into the individual to make him resourceful and self dependent. As such, it contained the seeds of true *Swaraj* or self rule, or democracy in the real sense of the term.[51] Thus whatever symbols Gandhi had chosen to lead the masses in the battle, to make the masses fit to achieve *Swaraj*. His meaning of democracy also intertwined with the right qualities in man like fearlessness, ability for self reliance, self realisation and motivation for selfless service. He was least concerned with institutional inputs to build democracy.

Similarly while speaking on religion Gandhi wanted to develop certain dormant qualities like fearlessness, *Brahmacharya*, control of the palate, nonstealing and nonpossession, bread labour, humility etc. in man. In the religious sphere these are the inputs necessary in a man to follow ethics. The main aim was to restructure man to suit to nonviolent society. To give a religious tinge Gandhi said that he was attempting to make man see divinity and thus subdue evil in him.

A look at the ideas of those commentators who looked at Gandhi as a man of God would clear certain amount of mist over Gandhi. One of the earliest associates of Gandhi, C.F. Andrews, was like Gandhi a savant of humanity and seeker of truth. The religious consciousness in him is both mystical and prophetic. He viewed Gandhi as a happy blend of faith and reason, and the spiritual and ethical. All this made him love the poor and the weak. This attracted him towards Gandhi. Hence while thinking about Gandhi, he considered Gandhi entirely 'Hindu' and supremely Christian. In other words Gandhi was a unique mixture of Hindu philosophy in search of Truth and Christian ethics professing love and compassion. At this stage religion and ritual has no place in Gandhian theology. This made Gandhi to steer clear of both religious 'right' and 'left'. To Gandhi religion means ethics and improvement of man. The man is the unit of measurement in evaluating all social values.

Mainly, Gandhites like K.G. Mashuriwala, Vinoba Bhave, Kaka Kalekar and Mahadev Desai looked at Gandhi in an exclusive angle of religion and theology. They interpreted Gandhi's ideas on religion in such a way that could see in Mahatma nothing but God as commonly understood. All these renowned people and a host of others who were near him tried to interpret Gandhi's ideas on religion and other related matters in the light of theology and theism. To them any ideology not connected with religion amounts to negation of ethics. They believed that religion alone could give moral foundation to every endeavour of man in his flight for perfection. This makes one's vision of Gandhi blurred. Gandhi on the other hand believed that religion is one of the instruments but not the sole instrument for effecting moral perfection in man. Here lies the fundamental difference between Gandhi and Gandhian over religion. Gandhi valued religion and wanted to convert it as an instrument to inject ethics in the individual to stir divinity, while Gandhian believed that religion is *sine qua non* for moral development. On the contrary in the absence of religion man cannot become an animal, for ethics govern his conduct. Gandhi believed in the infinite strength of man.

The difference between Gandhi and his religion soaked followers was that the former never looked at atheism as sin or as a creed like any other creed. As long as atheism propelled its adherents into action in wiping out tears from eyes of the poor and giving succour to them Gandhi respected and loved atheists. His respect and love for Gora can be cited as an illustration in this regard, while his followers labelled atheism and considered it on par with any labelled religion. As long as one serves his fellow beings with love and compassion Gandhi felt that his purpose was achieved. There is nothing much to dispute about.

Their main contention was that the adherents of atheism like Goparaju Rama Chandra Rao (Gora) always enthroned atheism and demolished everything in the hope that free will and principles of ethics are discounted. On the other hand both Gandhi and the atheists in the mould of Gora felt that service to man was important. Neither Gandhi nor atheists like Gora spoke of religion and God. Gandhi did not utter either religion or God when he advised to look into divinity in man. Divinity in man is more important to energise unlimited strength in man to remove evil. Similarly the adherents to atheism like Gora felt that the divinity outside the man is inhibiting the man himself to propel him into action. At this stage the evils associated with ritual crop up and make man inhibitive in approach. Purification of man is possible only when he realises that he can look into himself. This will lead to restructuring of man. It is essential to the evolution of nonviolent society. This is the main theme in Gandhian thought.

At the same time when one looks into the evolution of the meaning of God in Gandhian terms, the Gandhites felt that Gandhi had made the conception of God which is incomprehensible, made comprehensible. The unlimited and inexpressible God becomes limited and concrete. God becomes intelligible. At first Gandhi viewed that sum total of *Karma* is God. This *Karma* is selfless service. Next stage is love. Further evolution in Gandhi was God is Truth. And final culmination was Truth is God. Thus to some of the Gandhians, the incomprehensible unlimited the inexpressible God, had become comprehensible, limited and concrete in Gandhian lexicon. Out of sheer *Guru-Chela* relation between Gandhi and Ashramites the latter could not understand the former and his technique and purpose towards religion. Nor could subject him to searching questioning to penetrate into his mind. On the contrary they found alibies to support Mahatma in the conventional and conformist way. They failed to see clear streak of atheism in Gandhi. His theology covered this streak. The noise of the words God and religion in *Young India* and *Harijan* made them deaf. The sweet secular music remained unaudible and the purpose in Gandhian vocabulary remained unintelligible.

Because of mutually irreconcilable religious sects within *Hinduism* and religions on this land, genuine social reformers and freedom fighters did not give any importance to religion. Nor did they recognise the grip of religion over man for morality. To them religion was a hindrance to weld them into a nation. Therefore a social reformer like Gora or a freedom fighter like Bhagat Singh not only neglected religion but condemned labelled religions. Atheism is a sort of antidote to the grip of religion on disunity. Those who take an enlightened view of religion felt that atheism when assumes the role and colour of labelled religions it becomes worse.

In this context Gandhian views on conversion. missionary activity and communal harmony give a clear idea of religion which Gandhi held. To Gandhi religion means change of heart from sin to God.[52] And sin is defined as separation from God.[53] God is identified with Truth. Question of conversion does not arise. It is not conversion that is important. It is the effort of oneself to become a better Hindu if he is a Hindu, a better Muslim if he is a Muslim, and a better Christian if he is a Christian. In other words it is refining the individual by pushing towards ethics. Conversion drives the man from ethics and pushes towards sin. Conversion does not speak the language of heart. It speaks the language of mind the basis of selfishness. When Gandhi said that conversion is towards self-realisation and self-purification it means conversion from sin.

While speaking vehementally for communal harmony Gandhi preached that the individual must rise above fear, jealousy and hatred.[54] It is the panacea for communal harmony. Communal harmony is possible if one loves his religion respecting his neighbour's religion. The master key is to attempt to discover the underlying unity of all religions.[55] This unity is nothing but the ethics enunciated in every religion. He never believed any denominational religions. Gandhi wrote: "The need of the moment is not one religion, but mutual respect and tolerance of the devotees of the different religions. We want to reach not to the dead level, but unity in diversity. Any attempt that roots out traditions affects heredity, climate and other surroundings, is not only bound to fail, but is a sacrilege. The soul of religion is one, but it is encased in a multitude of forms. The latter will persist to the end of time. Wise men will ignore the outward crust and see the same soul living under variety of crusts."[56] Soul of religion is ethics or *vice-versa*. Therefore at a particular context Gandhi said: "Religion never suffers by reason of the criticism fair or foul of critics. It always suffers from the laxity or indifference of its followers."[57]

To a rationalist, experiences of mystics and seers appear as illusions and cannot be brought under scrutiny. Hence any religion and its effect are considered as secondary in the life of man. Whereas Gandhi took the crutches of religion to consolidate ethics in human life. While emphasising ethics and its importance, Gandhi felt the necessity of religion and says faith is a matter of heart and it appeals to the language of heart.[58] At this stage Gandhi followed a religious methods to preach a secular concept. Whereas an atheist in his zeal for a social purpose discards the methods inherent in religion. In the process he leaves religion as of no consequence. Gandhi, as he adopted religious methods to reach his goal appeared more a theist than an atheist.

A believer in God and religion speaks of psychic limitations in comprehending God, while a nonbeliever thinks illusion created by religion has to be destroyed for generating human initiative to wipe out obscurantist ideas. Gandhi was neither an obscurantist nor suffered any psychic limitations. His principle was selfless action and self-realisation. His concept of these two had been identified with theology, whereas these two, to others are not theological concepts. Selflessness and self realisation aim at individual improvement alone without any reference to society and human environment. These two get a tinge of theology. This aspect cannot be traced in Gandhian thought, if not altogether absent.

The entire concept of atheism as opposed to theism generates self confidence and free thinking unfettered by the chains of something unknown as religion. Similarly a theist maintains that one gets inner strength through religion. Once inner strength develops it becomes basis for self-confidence and free will. What was the position of Gandhi vis-a-vis these two stands ? Gandhi's mission was to turn the individual to recognise the power of divinity inside him. Once divinity is recognised evil in him gets subdued. The path for nonviolent society gets cleared. Truth and the divinity in life will not only be felt but respected. Nonviolence and approach to Truth are means to an end. The end is the removal of exploitation. Theism, the belief in God and religion, atheistic concept of realisation of nonviolent society, revolve round to give meaning to life which survives amidst death and destruction.

What is Truth ? To an atheist or an agnoistic truth is a relative idea. Absolute truth is beyond the comprehension of any atheist or agnoistic. It is because of the influence of his experience and his background. Similar may be the case with Gandhi also. Truth to any person means what he himself feels and knows to be true. Then what is truth according to Gandhi ? What he felt ? What he saw in this world? He felt some unseen energy which propels the world towards a forward movement. In the words of Gandhi it is 'Godward'. What does it mean? A constant knocking at the heart of man to look at the life through the heart but not through the mind. This 'Godward' movement oozes with love and compassion. In its train it brings nonviolence and recognises as the only means to remove agony and misery from human relations. This will lead to the recognition of the sanctity of human life at a preliminary stage. And at the final stage it is the sanctity of all life.

As per Gandhians, atheists in negating God and religion are not pursuing any noble ideas. Their aim to improve society does not hold any ground. Godlessness is immoral. Now the question is: Is Godlessness immoral? If not immoral is there any positive content in atheistic thought? An atheist is as much dependent on his ism as a votary of any labelled religion. Denial of God becomes first premise in the thinking of an atheist before knowing what God is. Negation of God on the part of atheists blinds them to see limitless energy and infallibility of man to improve himself. Self realisation and selfless service constitute the corner stone of the Gandhian ethics for the improvement of man which according to Gandhians cannot find place in atheism or no God state of mind. On this basis Gandhians feel that in a no God society self realisation and selfless service are not possible. Similarly in a no God society morals may not be present as lay understand. There is no possibility of recognising divinity in man.

Gandhi recognised self in man. Felt the possibility of constant refinement of self or soul at every moment. With the atheists self means the human being himself with a desire to live forever. Only when one is clear of self he is towards 'Godward'. Gandhi was somewhere between these two extremes. He recognised self and its importance unlike atheists. After this recognition he felt the importance of self to work according to one's own conscience for the betterment of society, where there will not be any restriction of free will and thinking. In the eyes of an atheist self is a moral human body desiring to live. In the absence of fetters in the form of religion human being is free to think and act as per the conscience. Now these two schools of thought are clear in their approaches towards the common aim.

Gandhi took the theistic medium to convey his thoughts but at the same time remained free from religion and ritual.

Another fallacy on the part of theists is that there cannot be any discussion on nonexistence or existence of God. It is because man is still ignorant of himself. Hence the first and only condition is that the one is made eligible to discuss the existence and nonexistence of God. Further he is made to be aware of himself. Had Gandhi understood the man? The question is pertinent and important. Answer is yes. He understood man and found in him indefinite energy and infallibility to improve himself into a better man, a better Hindu, a better Muslim, a better Christian etc. While discovering divinity in man, Gandhi discarded the ritual and form of religion. To him religion is an external stimulant for ethics in man while limiting God to truth for the sake of comprehension, he saw truth in the limitless possibility to improve man. All this drives us to the conclusion that Gandhi was least bothered to define religion or God. He was a rebel and a revolutionary. Spoke to the masses in the idiom they could follow.

When religion and philosophy get mixed, a calm confluence of these two mighty rivers takes place, where man has to search his self to float on this confluence. A right understanding of the self alone gives guidance and thrust to the man to move forward i.e. 'Godward'. The word self attracted the theist as well as the atheist. The former achieved his attempt to immortality with the help of the concept of soul. An atheist thinks that with the unfolding of truth on the physical plane perpetuation of immortality is possible. In other words he wants to achieve immortality with the help of truth. Gandhi never looked into these two aspects. Accepted the theistic logic in the refinement of soul and thus of man. His purpose was to inculcate ethics in man. The theistic logic served Gandhi's purpose. At every stage of development man goes a step towards selflessness and self realisation. This entire logic of Gandhi indirectly robs anything remotely connected with the concept of God, when he said the movement to 'Godward' is progress.

On the basis of logic atheists quarrel with theists. God is incomprehensible. For every comprehensible term there is an opposite term. Because God is incomprehensible, there is no comprehensible opposite term of God. Only when God is made comprehensible man can invent a comprehensible term to God. When Gandhi said :

'Truth is God', it is generally felt that an attempt was made to project God in comprehensible terms. Thus Gandhi was imperceptibly leaning towards atheistic streak in him, which was coveted by unlimited quantum of theistic words Gandhi used. This made him inconsistent and contradictory. This was one of the main reasons he was contradicting himself knowingly with a deliberate push towards a set goal viz. convincing man to look into himself for his inherent capability of infinite development. In this pilgrimage labelled religion with its ritual and priest craft was thrown over board.

What is the aim of an atheist? His quarrel is not with God. God is incomprehensible to the atheist as well as to the theist. His quarrel is with those people who in the name of God exploit the gullible, the weak and the meek. A true theist softens man, tries to control the animal in man. But as long as religion and priest become the exclusive possession of the privileged and the strong in society religion produces inertia in man and opens flood gates of exploitation. Gandhian technique was to remove this animal in man. Gandhi was well aware of the fact that the rich and the strong cannot be dispossessed of religion and priest. At the same time he knew that the average man who is seeped in religion cannot be made to listen to him unless he coats his concepts and ideas that are vital for the improvement of man and his environment with theistic coat. At this stage Gandhian politics, economics, sociology and theology converge and present a unique picture of Gandhi. Thus Gandhi was a right mixture of a politician, an economist, a social reformer, a seer and a philosopher. Hence a closer examination and analysis of Gandhi are required. The question is not whether Gandhi is relevant today? The question is in what proportion of politician, economist, social reformer, theist, seer and philosopher in Gandhi required to society. The answer is clear. Gandhian thought spiritualises every aspect of man.

In theology and philosophy one cannot declare a final word, since the truth is not fully unwrapped. At the most a look at Gandhi's aim which may clear the mist over Gandhian thought. What is the Gandhian conception of God and religion? No definite answer is possible. Hence final word eludes. Gandhi did not venture to explain what God is. Neither did he feel the necessity for the explanation. To him "God is beyond human comprehension"[59] He placed importance on sincere, selfless activity mitigating agony in human life. In this context Gandhi while appreciating Gora told him: "Atheism is a denial of self. No one has propagated it. Such success as you (Gora) have attained is due to your sincere work among the people round you. I am sorry I cannot invite you to come here. I have no time to spare for talks."[60] On the contrary Gora believed that denial of self is not there in his atheism. And his is the assertion on self.[61] It was his total devotion to work made Gandhi to see merit in Gora. He was invited in 1944 to Sevagram. His effort of knocking at the doors of Gandhi since 1931 bore fruit. The mutual attraction between these two saw selfless work towards the betterment of the under dog. Gandhi saw in his God the selfless work and suffering of Gora. Similarly Gora could see his own God from the throne : enthroned selfless work and ceaseless activity. This was the magnetic feed to draw Gandhi towards Gora. Atheism was not the bond between the two. It is the selfless work and the common aim of the both. At this stage means and end controversy did not haunt Gandhi. Gora applied atheism as operational principle in his work. While Gandhi preached that the recognition of divinity in man is necessary to appreciate sanctity of life as the sole principle of his work. It is clear that Gandhi never considered atheism as a block for his ethical religion. He found besides the selfless work in the mission of Gora, his humility, which reduced him to nothing to see divinity in man. Hence he could see God in his ameliorating effort. Though the end was identical in the case of Gandhi and Gora, the means differed outwardly. The former adopted a theistic interpretation of his secular ideas to achieve his purpose, while the latter took a atheistic stick to lean on to reach his goal. Though the means differed Gandhi had to have a second look at Gora. Why? Atheism is not immoral if selfless service becomes the motto.

In the beginning, Gora and his atheism were discarded by Gandhi as he was too theoretical to action. But Gora proved that an atheistic outlook broke the barriers of the caste, the barriers between the man and woman and the religious barriers, seeing the communal riots and the blood bath that our country had, Gandhi "wished the communalist turned atheists if that served to stop communal hatred and riots."[62] This is the beginning and end in seeing ethics in atheism on the part of Gandhi. Theism and atheism were not the dominant themes in Gandhi. The dominant theme is selfless service with humility to see truth in the life amidst death. Life has to be protected

This is the ethos of nonviolence. Violence creates violence destroying everything. Nonviolence protects life amidst death and destruction. The truth which is God to Gandhi was the existence of life. Truth not only binds man to man in a social organisation but also "a means of existence, the existence of that we know and of that we do not know. The sum total of all existence is absolute truth or the truth."[63] The origin and the growth of life in some aspects is visible to everyone. The invisible aspect of life is equally important if not more. The invisibility forms the part of the energy that keeps momentum of life. In the totality of life Gandhi saw his God : Truth, agony and anguish are reduced if nonviolence is taken as operating principle in changing the pattern of relationships to assist the change or movement of the world for progress. The greater the intensity of nonviolence the lesser the pain and misery. In the course of discussion with Gora on truth and the significance attached to the words like 'Raghupathi Raghav' Gandhi proudly declared that he was a 'super atheist' what does it mean ? The answer is simple. It means he was capable of throwing God, religion and atheistic principles away in preference to self improvement to become an effective instrument for selfless service. "Gandhi was pre-eminently a practical man"[64] and humanitarian.[65]

While discussing with Gora on atheism, Gora pointed out that atheism is a tonic for self confidence. And it will lead to the establishment of social and economic friction free structure, Gandhi appreciated sincerity and conviction of Gora. And he said "Yes I see an ideal in your talk. I can neither say my theism is right and your atheism is wrong. We are seekers after truth. We change where we find ourselves in the wrong. I changed like that many a time in my life. I see you are a worker. you are not a fanatic. You will change whenever you find yourself in the wrong. There is no harm as long as you are not fanatical whether you are in the right or I am in the right, results will prove. Then I may go your way or you may come my way, or both of us may go a third way. So go ahead with your work. I will help you though your method is against me."[66] Even Gandhi's followers could see in Gora the glow which blazes the path of selfless service. Kishorilal Mashuriwala wrote while discussing Gora's ideas, "His atheistic doctrines might change with the advancement of thought and experience, or might get more firmly set in course of time. This depends upon several factors. But as long as he retains a loving heart, exemplary moral character and courage, both in personal and public life, and a life of service and sacrifice, his will be found in the list of God's own devotees. For his sake *Deva* will assume the name of *Adeva*."[67] This is the essence of Gandhian thought on theology.

Gandhi was primarily a man of action to energise the weak to fight against injustice and exploitation. In his teaching God and religion are absent. He tried to pacify the individual with his ideas of truth and nonviolence. But this pacification is not submission.[68] It is nonsubmission to wrongs in society. As a pacifist he trained his masses to accept infinite pain and suffering. As a *satyagrahi* he trained them to hold on to the truth, though capable to fight, taught them to stick to nonviolence. It is because in Gandhi's scheme of action one does not hate his opponent. At the same time loves his adversary. Though his methods were followed by a pacifist, he was activist full of dynamic energy. He was not concerned with theories and theoretical discussions. He was solely concerned to steel the moral fibre in man to accept pain and suffering with an attitude of total nonsubmission. This is the technique to make one a rebel against injustice. His constructive programme is based on selfless service and self-realisation. As a rebel he did not find in theology any relevance to his programme of action. Theology had no utility in his constructive programme. At this stage his ideas on religion, God, theism, ethics and above all his secular ideas got mixed up into a chemical compound. Analysis and examination become extremely difficult. Further his experiments with truth put him on the road to growth and progress. Every moment he was picking up correct things, correcting his ideas and shaping them to suit to the results of his experiments. Therefore, though, atheism as a word odium to Ashramites as well as his audience he could boldly call himself a 'super atheist'. This epitomises his entire technique of speaking to his masses intelligibly i.e. conveying secular ideas through theistic medium. Thus Gandhi became a super communicator of his secular ideas without allowing the 'God stunt' distort his concepts.

REFERENCES

1. *Harijan*, 30 May, 1936.
2. *Ibid.*
3. *Ibid.*

4. *Harijan*, 6 March, 1937.
5. *Hindu Dharma*, : Navajivan Publishing House, Ahmedabad 1950, p.184.
6. *Op. cit.*, p. 223.
7. *Hindu Dharma*, p.190.
8. *Ibid.*
9. *Ibid.*
10. *Op. cit.*, p.105.
11. Dr. Iswar Tope. *Ethos of Non-violence*, Navajivan Publishing House, Ahmedabad, 1964, p. 40.
12. *Hindu Dharma*, p. 250.
13. *Harijan*, 24 August, 1934.
14. *Ibid.*
15. *Ibid.*
16. *Harijan*, 3 Oct., 1936.
17. *Ibid.*
18. *Harijan*, 3 Oct., 1936.
19. *Harijan*, 24 Aug., 1934.
20. *Harijan*, 16 Dec., 1939.
21. *Young India*, 6 Aug. 1931.
22. *Ibid.*
23. *Ibid.*
24. *Ibid.*
25. *Ibid.*
26. *Ibid.*
27. *Ibid.*
28. *Ibid.*
29. *Young India*, 22 Sept., 1927.
30. *Ibid.*
31. *In Search of the Supreme*, Vol. III, p. 231.
32. *Op. cit.*, p. 239.
33. *Op. cit.*, p. 245.
34. *Op. cit.*, p. 317.
35. K.L. Sheshagiri Rao, *Mahatma Gandhi and C.F. Andrews*. Punjab University, Patiala, 1969, p. 33.
36. M.K. Gandhi : *Satyagraha in South Africa*, Navajivan Publishing House: Second Edition Ahemedabad, 1950, p. 73.
37. *Op. cit.*, p. 45.
38. *Op. cit.*, p. 102.
39. *Op. cit.*, p. 105.
40. *Op. cit.*, pp. 105, 106.
41. *Op. cit.*, p. 147.
42. *Op. cit.*, p. 168.

43. *Op. cit.*, p. 169.
44. *Op. cit.*, p. 212.
45. *Harijan*, 27 May, 1939.
46. *Ibid.*
47. *Harijan*, 20 Jan., 1940.
48. *Harijan*, 23 March, 1947.
49. *Ibid.*
50. *Harijan*, 25 Oct., 1952.
51. M.K. Gandhi : *Khadi*, Ed. Bharatan Kumarappa Editorial Note, pp. III, IV.
52. *Harijan*, 28 Sep., 1935.
53. *Ibid.*
54. *Harijan*, 1 Dec. 1946.
55. *Harijan*, 13 July, 1940.
56. *Young India*, 25 Sep., 1924.
57. *Harijan*, 3 Nov., 1946.
58. *Young India*, 23 April, 1931.
59. In a letter to Gora in 1930 : Quoted in Gora ; *An Atheist with Gandhi*, Navajeevan Publishing House, Ahmedabad 1951 : p. 26.
60. *Op. cit.*, p. 27.
61. *Ibid.*
62. *Op. cit.*, p. 50.
63. *Op. cit.*, p. 48.
64. *Op. cit.*, p. 35.
65. *Op. cit.*, p. 59.
66. *Op. cit.*, p. 44.
67. *Op. cit.*, p. 24.
68. Jawaharlal Nehru, *Mahatma Gandhi*, Asia Publishing House, 1949, p. 17.

6

Religion Reversed

FROM the beginning Gandhi's contact with religion developed scepticism rather than veneration of and faith in religion. He was born in a family that adored *Vaishnav* faith. Very often he visited *Haveli* with his parents and elders. But it never appealed to him. Its glitter and pomp did not attract him much. He did not like it. He heard the rumours of immorality practised there. He abhored these. He lost interest. His nurse an old maid servant at home with her affection towards him inculcated the practice of repetition of *Ramanama.* He developed faith in *Ramanama.* It all began to drive away the fear of ghosts and spirits. He learnt *Ramayana* and *Rama Raksha.* He was acquainted with the *Bhagavad.* With his parents he used to visit Shiva's and Rama's temples. Gradually tolerance to all branches of Hinduism sprouted in him. To add to this very frequently Jain monks visited his father. They even accepted food from them. Gandhi used to listen to their talks with his father on religion and other related matters. He used to listen and talk to his Muslim and Parsi friends of their faith. Except Christianity he came to know other faiths.

All these things did not produce requisite faith in God.[1] He had a living faith in God. He further told that *Manusmriti* did not impress him.[2] The story of creation and similar things in it did not stir him to faith. On the contrary he was made to incline towards atheism.[3] The atheistic streak in him further captivated him. Whenever the young Gandhi tried to get his doubts clarified he did not get any satisfactory answer. He was told that he would understand as he grew old. Gandhi also had assured himself saying : "With intellect more developed and with more reading I shall understand it better."[4] Still the young Gandhi remained free from the grip of faith. There were no incidents through which he passed that could have inculcated faith and belief in the potency of religion. He remained sceptic. The *Ramanama* that served as an antidote from the fear of ghosts and spirits had gone into his psyche. This may be the reason for him at a later stage to propagate *Ramanama* not as a religious *mantra* but as a resonant reasoning the body. From the beginning, may be due to the environment charged with morals Gandhi developed a conviction that morality is the basis of things and that truth is the substance of all morality.[5] Thus truth became his sole objective. "It began to grow in magnitude every day and his definition of it also has been ever widening."[6] His definition of truth and later his understanding of it became the sole reference point of his comprehension of religion and God. Accordingly his conception of religion and God is at variance. Even his concept of faith and wisdom revolves round his understanding of the truth. His truth was the meeting place of a theist as well as an atheist who could see the radiance of their images. At a very tender age foundation for morality and truth was laid in him. In his autobiography he quoted a Gujarati didactic stanza that gripped his mind.[7] Its precept return good for evil became his guiding principle.[8] This may be the initial step to see good in man and the power of good over evil. Evil can be reduced in man and ultimately wiped out.

These moral principles always held his imagination. Ethics totally gripped him. The result was Gandhi developed a theology based on ethics. Ethics touch the inner core of man and purify him. In a theistic language it means man is spiritualised. He is no longer a menace to his environment. On the contrary he is an effective instrument to creativity amidst destruction and death. The evolution of society unfolds without the birth pangs. "For a while he was practically an atheist. Upto that point he had worshipped the gods honestly. He had never, since the age of reasoning, imagined that the stone or wood or metal image was itself a God, but he had been told and believed that an act of consecration endowed the image with a divine spirit and this localised spirit he worshipped. His companionship with other minds, however, almost imperceptibly changed his conception of religion. He became sceptical. A strong natural tendency to analytical study made him question the why of every thing."[9] With this critical mind he had probed the basis of religion and its purpose. His analysis led him to believe that when ethics become the basis, the purpose for which religion is created will be clear. With this critical bent of mind he probed religion, educated the fanatics and found the unity of all religions. But he never considered religion alone as the panacea for the removal of evils in man and society. At this stage as a social scientist he evolved a method and scheme for the progressive evolution of society. With this aim and purpose, Gandhi gradually textured a pattern of life for himself which his followers felt religious. Whenever the pattern did not suit to the description of religion as commonly understood, the follower tried to stretch the meaning of religion as wide as possible to encompass the concepts and precepts of Gandhi in religion. These were dyed in religious line and with religious terminology. A deft analysis is required to free Gandhi from the religious weeds. Only then a set pattern of Gandhi's scheme and method would emerge.

A look at Gandhi will reveal many things. He was a crusader against oppression. He was a rebel against the prevailing order, where justice was hardly found. He was a social reformer. He was a political strategist. He was an economist assuring food and employment. He involved the masses in political movement. Thus he became the radical of the radicals. He chose appropriate symbols and adopted these to catch the imagination of the masses in his battle against colonialism. His social reform touched every aspect to bring out the best in man without dismantling social institutions. Hence at the surface he gave the appearance of a conservative. But he was an out and out a nonconformist. In the social and religious fields he touched only those problems which if ignored would bring misery and calamity. Communal harmony and the removal of untouchability engaged his attention always. These two had to be annihilated with all the might at his command. Because, these two stood in the way of integrating our country. At the same time in his scheme of things these two if perpetuated the evil in man cannot be removed. They have a peculiar significance to India and a wider import to the survival of mankind. He never rested before these two problems. His entire socio-political and religious philosophy was revolved round these two problems. It has a wider connotation. If these two problems get solved, automatically his scheme of things unfold. He had never spoken anything which might stand in the way of removing these aberrations from this soil.

From the point of scepticism Gandhi moved to a stage where he was considered as a 'man of God' and 'man of religion'. This transformation or it would be appropriate to say journey was at a steady pace. His *ashramites* and through them masses could not see anything in him except religion. Gandhi on the other hand knew the weakness of his followers. He advocated secular ideas in theistic jargon to the intellectuals and in theistic idiom to the masses. He could serve his purpose. From the external point of view his ability for organisation and his clarion call captured the imagination of the country. This made him a leader, a revolutionary and a rebel. But his real greatness lies in his spiritual qualities through which a social philosophy was envisioned. It is both a system of philosophy and plan of action to achieve the aim set.

Gandhi reached a stage where action oriented people are attracted towards him. They might have been theists, atheists and agnoistic. He created place only to those who were counted for activity alone. Two things are very striking in this direction. Gandhi at the outset emphasised an altruistic activity. What is its relation with religion? Or more specifically what is the objective of spiritual destination? In mundane terms it may be helping the needy. Suffering and misery are man made. These have to be removed. This is one aspect of the problem. In spiritual matters more work alone does not lead anywhere even though it is an unselfish work. From this stage the second stage arrives. The second stage is to gradually train man to effect detachment from the bondage of matter. These two stages when coupled together the foundation for higher spiritual values is laid. This was exactly what Gandhi had been advocating and doing. People saw in him more of his spiritual aspect, even though it was devoid of theology.

In Gandhi these two aspects took deep root. An individual however intellectual he may be, and be capable of intellectual discussion and discourse of religious principles and doctrines, if his thoughts and actions continue to be impure and selfish, the attainment of religious values become very remote and even impossible. Keeping this yardstick one has to look at Mahatma. He was religious yet different from the people visiting a temple, a church or a mosque. He was different from people who go on pilgrimage. He was also different from those who take a holy dip in the Ganga or in some other river sanctified because it is mentioned in the epics. Yet he was more religious than these. What made him a religious man without religious trappings? Though he did not believe in any religious denomination he is acclaimed as the individual who could attain highest spiritual values. This phenomenon is unique and novel.

To unravel this marvel one has to look into the activities of Gandhi, whether in his war for independence, or making people self-sufficient, or welding the country into a nation, or training the people for activity. He always tried to achieve spiritual idealism in all his activities. Expedience never dominated in his calculations and plan of action. Success was not the criterion. It is spiritual idealism that dominated his actions and decisions. His aim was always to stir divinity or divine qualities in man to remove the evil in opponent. He had always tried to purify the systems and institutions not at the cost of man but at the removal of evil in him. This power of spirit kept Gandhi free from the contamination. He was totally insulated by the power of spiritual values. He was conscious about the divinity in man. This lifted his political work to the level of spiritual work. Hypocracy and diplomacy never touched his work. His aim was not only to lead the people to *Swaraj* but to educate the people of what *Swaraj* is and make them fit for *Swaraj*. The selfish interest or interested behaviour is not only to be curbed and has to be removed altogether in all activity.

Gandhi's conception of *Swaraj* was different from the mere attainment of *Swaraj*. His politics never contemplated to serve selfish ends of the people engaged. No doubt in the Gandhian calculations the immediate aim was to wrest freedom from the British. But in the post freedom era no individual or particular class or community should exploit others for selfish ends. Further he tried to make people fearless to resist authority if it deviated from morals. Thus his actions were altruistic and beneficial to the others. If this is translated in theological terms it means spiritual values.

In priority wise after *Swaraj*, self-sufficiency occupies important place in his scheme of things. Individual has to be trained to become self-sufficient. He should not be dependent upon others for his needs. At every stage the individual should be strengthened. This is possible only when he is refined. His divine qualities have to be tapped. He should be made to feel strong and bold. This is possible only when he is free from the bondage of material things and gets himself bonded to work. This instils stamina, confidence, faith, in oneself and courage in him. Dynamism is produced. Put the individual on a trial for self sacrifice.

The individual should be action oriented. His action is not only result oriented, but also should be evaluated in the light of spiritual values. This will guide him in his acts between the true and false and between the pure and impure. Our vision of truth gets distorted due to our selfishness and personal likes and dislikes. This is one of the reasons the seekers of spiritual life remain in seclusion. But this was not the method that Gandhi preferred. He wanted the individual to be an active participant in the society he lives. At the same time he has to cultivate the immunity from the influences and temptations. This will have two advantages. Firstly one's action can produce the required thrust and secondly the individual will be able to follow the right course where the evil in him gets subdued. The result will be that work gets hue of worship and man will be on the path of self purification.

Next important aspect that Gandhi wanted his *Ashramites* to practise humility. In front of the others one has to reduce himself to nothing to learn the things. This makes one to see clearly divinity in others. And there will be interaction between the two. With this humility one approaches religious lore the ethical content rich and varied in it can be picked up. At this stage it is not ritual, rite or priest or *mahant* that gives spiritual sustenance, but the ethical content embedded in scriptures and the philosophy behind religion give armour to man to remain strong, bold and free from fear.

Gandhi began his journey as a sceptic. In his march he saw the immense strength in man. This can be achieved by subduing evil in man. To make man invincible he chalked out a programme to be followed. When Gandhi followed his programme to convince his opponent that his acts were against injustice without hating him, people around him saw his love and compassion, the sparks of divinity in him and unfolding of kingdom of God in him. This radiance blinded the others. Instead of humanism they saw theology. The entire process was a sort of reverse action. It is not faith and wisdom that made Gandhi look like a religious *messiah*. It is his scepticism, his reasoning attitude, his spirit of enquiry, his faith in man for his growth and progress that made him a sort of religious person to his *Ashramites* and comon masses. His nonviolence and truth are the means and end of his philosophy. Stir the divinity in man he will be reformed and will assist the movement of the world towards truth. Remove the friction with the help of the creed of nonviolence. Then misery and agony are reduced. In this endeavour religion was used by Gandhi as a symbol but not as an instrument.

Gandhi was head and shoulders above the other great men who had engineered the struggle for freedom and led the masses to freedom in the early part of the present century. In the matters of spiritual no great leader could be compared with him. How he achieved these heights? The road was not through religion and faith. The road was through scepticism and wisdom. He was observed. He was followed closely. Divinity in him attracted everyone—the lay and the intellectual, sceptic and faithful and the follower and the opponent. He became a Mahatma. He achieved this by reversing religion. His ethical religion got content and significance because of its social purpose and the recognition of man as the centre of society.

REFERENCES

1. M.K. Gandhi, *An Autobiography or the Story of My Experiments with Truth.* Navajivan Publishing House, Ahmedabad. Third Edition : 1982, p. 29.
2. *Ibid.*
3. *Ibid.*
4. *Ibid.*
5. *Ibid.*
6. *Ibid.*
7. *Op. cit.*, p. 30.
8. *Ibid.*
9. Joseph. J. Doke : *M.K. Gandhi : An Indian Patriot in South Africa,* Publications Division : 1967, New Delhi, p. 29.

7

POSTSCRIPT

"FRAGILE and fugitive" human life requires a system which supplies meaning, value and vital to human life. It was Gandhi who devised a system that contributes the meaning, value and vitality to human existence. Man can live with an aim and mission in life if he follows this Gandhian system. Life has two parts: seen and unseen parts. When these two get fused into one, the vision into human life gets blurred. The result is innumerable ideologies and religious formats come into play over the man. He gets confused and bewildered. He is at a loss to know what to do. The void is filled with misery and agony out of frustration. This weakness in man had been exploited in the past and at present it is being exploited. And credulous minds become prey to this exploitation that goes in the name of religion and spirituality.

Fertile human intellect probes into the unseen or unknowable part of human life, to know the reality. Intellect cannot deliver the goods. Hence faith takes its place. Faith may not be based on individual experience and in some cases may be based on experience. Individual experience is not supported by verification. Faith therefore becomes sheet anchor of the unseen part of human life. In this realm faith probes into reality. Consequently the individual is dependent upon religion. Unfortunately no religious creed or system adequately if not clearly analysed so far the unknown parts of human existence. Therefore theology became canonical. Religion has a role to play. But when the grip of religion fails to inspire the individual, he leans towards liberalism or liberal tendencies. Thus the slogan is for liberation of theology.

Did Gandhi give anything new in the realm of theology? Or did he contribute toward liberal theology ? To the first question the answer is 'Yes' and to the second one the answer is 'No'. He was not a man for any denominational religion nor labelled religion. Hence the question of liberation does not arise as far as Gandhism is concerned. He had a vision of human existence. Hence whatever he had spoken and written in the sphere of religion or more precisely on the unseen part of human existence constitute a system to know the unknowable.

There is always continuity and change in the human existence. It is evolution if analysed. This evolution is not only mere the result of the play of natural and physical laws over the individual and his environment, but also the urge and effort of the individual to shape himself and be an effective instrument in making his fragile and fugitive existence into a strong contribution was immense and novel.

In this effort of the individual, before the advent of politics and economics as full fledged systems of study with the other social sciences, philosophy as a search for truth became handy. In its search for truth philosophy followed certain facts and stimulated thinking to search for meaning of this captive existence. He looked at the saints and seers whose consciousness is wider and deeper. Felt confident of himself. It gives some respite to him. Tries to find sweetness and light. The meaning of the unknown part sometimes appear in flickers. Gets satisfied. At this stage, experience gets blended with faith. Where the effort for change and continuity touches the known parts of human life the thought takes the ruts of politics and economics to fashion the human life. The result is ceaseless effort to refashion the environment. The individual is hardly touched. He is left alone. The philosophic part of the thought that peeps into the unknown part of the human life, when fails to satisfy the intellect, man to know this takes refuge under religion.

What is the aim of life? How continuity is maintained and what changes are required? Aim is creativity and it has to be increased amidst destruction. Preservation of life amidst death. The sacredness of life is more important. It is the carrier for creativity. In essence it means refinement of the human being. It aims at liberty and happiness for the individual. A look at the growth testifies this. The growth was steadily in the beginning from inorganic to organic. Next from organic to sentient. Later from sentient to rational. Rationality always pushed man not to get himself coiled with the thought that is current, and frees him from rupturous amazement at the things which he did not know hitherto. This rationality enables him to search new paths for liberation and happiness. In terms of religion liberation denotes exploration of human being himself. It is knowing self. Happiness means removal of violence on the path of evolution.

The problem of liberation and happiness as opposed to hedonism can be understood if a search is made on the spiritual landscape. According to the *Upanishads, Brahamvidya* or *Atma Vidya* is necessary to rationalise the human existence. It is not to run away from life. It is not to avoid the pains in existence. It is to evolve a system for improvement. This improvement is towards 'Godward'. In the *Katha Upanishad* the teaching is that the individual should be free from the iron grip of senses. It makes the individual insulated from power and possession. He gets himself reduced to nothing. He becomes as pure as an infant's body ready to be injected for vitalisation. The goodness in him expands. Heart dominates intellect. Thus the conquering of self and attainment of enlightenment are possible. These two aspects are corner stones of Jainism and Buddhism besides Hinduism. Similarly in Islam the emphasis of conduct over creed is there. It will be clear when a distinction is made between Islam and Mohammadanism. These teachings push the individual towards the spiritual adventure of knowing oneself. Though Gandhi talked about self-realisation, his search of reality more specifically his experiments with truth confined to know the divinity in man. This divinity is nothing but good in man. In Christianity the realization of 'kingdom of God within' conforms the broad sweep of Eastern religions.

Thus religion as a system in its search for the meaning in the unknown part of the human life puts him on the trail of *Brahma* within. This philosophical content is theology. It is the mirror to all the labelled religions to know the beauty of the awareness of self. But unfortunately the votaries of all these religions suffer from their limited knowledge. The ritual and the creed became the centre point of their systems. They failed to accord right place to the individual. Their lack of awareness of the individual, as the centre of the universe makes them fall prey to illusions. Finality of the existing knowledge is the main illusion in front of them. This makes the way for fanaticism. In this context Gandhi raised the slogan to become a better Hindu, a better Muslim, so that the individual is not a helpless spectator before the illusion that is produced by the thought of finality of knowledge at a given time. Thus Gandhi gave a new turn and content to theological thought. This illusion always stands on the way of human progress.

This illusion becomes a reality to all religious creeds. Unfortunately secular ideologies also become the victims of this illusion. The adherents of these creeds and ideologies think that their knowledge is final. The blocks are not demolished. The result is that all these creeds and ideologies are soaked in blood. Misery and agony dance with vigour and rhytam. To mitigate this Gandhi came forward with his nonviolence. It shows hope to mankind to bring succour to the poor and to give sanity to the mighty.

The need for liberation and happiness is a perpetual craving on the part of the individual. It is based on the fact that man suffers from inward loneliness. A constant fear haunts him. He feels helpless. He finds no happiness amidst material comfort. Further his growth is marked with birth pangs and again pangs of adjustments with his environment at every turn of transition. He finds at a loss to know what is development. All this makes him seek liberation from his captive existence. He seeks happiness at every turn in his transition towards growth.

What is the cause for this inward loneliness. The root cause is fear and hatred. At every turn of transition self-aggrandization takes place. The fear of losing his importance and the fear that the fellow being may surpass leads to hatred along with fear. These two may become the cause of his annihilation ultimately. With all his, achievement in literature, arts and civilization man is nowhere in his pursuit of happiness. On the contrary he may be nearing his extinction. Civilization disappears leaving signs in the form of fossils. Reality seems to allude him with the gain of more and more control over nature. As he increases his power of destruction to annihilate the fellow being because of his hatred, he approaches to the brink of self destruction. With the wrapping of the earth with star war the hitherto powerful missiles became obsolete. Thus man is guided in his planned suicide. Theology speaks of cosmic process to lead the man to pre-determined goal as per the plan of God. This theological determinism does not bestow any importance to man. He ramains always in search of ways and means to be free from fear and to seek happiness.

Man gradually rolls on towards self destruction because of his love for self aggrandizement and hatred. Theology that speaks of cosmic process to guide the man to a predetermined destination does not offer any system by which he may not be driven towards self extinction. Man's intellect fans the embers of fear and hatred. A prophet or a seer takes off despair in man. Injects love into him for the others. Thus individual is made fit to drive out fear and to love others. At this stage relevance of Gandhi is felt. Even in future his relevance will remain to make man struggle for perpetual peace. Urge for perpetual peace lingers on as the inner voice of man. Gandhi recognised this strength of inner voice in man which hinges on divinity in him. The stronger the divinity in man the quicker the attainment of peace. But unfortunately the conflict is between the conscious purpose of man and his unconscious impulse of fear and hatred. The divinity in man according to Gandhi lies in his compassion and nobility. At his worst man is full of hatred. Thus he is a compound of both good and evil. The more the evil dominated him the more fear engulfs him resulting into hatred. Hatred releases the energy for self-extinction. The more divinity asserts the man his conscious purpose of reaching towards cosmic determinism possible, which Gandhi had said 'Godward'.

In this frame where did Gandhi stand ? "Gandhi was essentially a man of religion, a Hindu to the inner most depths of being and yet his conception of religion had nothing to do with any dogma or custom or ritual."[1] He remained a Hindu not because he was born a Hindu. The philosophical content of the *Vedas* and the *Upanishads* brought rationality to the theology. He believed in this rational character. His belief in moral law was further strengthened with the backing of the Hindu books. To him moral law is the basis of his religion. His entire attempt was to refine man injecting ethics into him. While commenting on Hinduism Gandhi wrote: "Hinduism is a living organism liable to growth and decay, and subject to laws of nature. One and indivisible at the root it has grown into a vast tree with innumerable branches. The changes in the seasons affect it. It has its autumn and summer, its winter and spring. The rains nourish and fructify it too. It is and is not based on scriptures. It does not derive its authority from one book. The *Gita* is universally accepted, but even then it only shows the way. Even like the Ganges it is beneficient in its total effect. It takes a provincial form in every province, but the inner substance is retained everywhere. Custom is not religion, religion will remain unaltered."[2] Thus Gandhi never believed in the finality of knowledge. He found in Hinduism not only the moral principles but a way of thinking to explore unlimited knowledge. "Hinduism abhors stagnation. Knowledge is limitless and so also the application of truth."[3] This aspect of Hinduism attracted Gandhi most. In Hinduism he found confluence of truth in the *Vedas* and the philosophic-cum-ethical content. There is no place for fear and hatred in Hinduism. To Gandhi. "Hinduism is more a culture than a creed". The dogma, the creed, and the ritual had no place in his scheme of things. He did not want to become a slave to any teaching. His path was clear and his vehicle was nonviolence. Religion has to satisfy inner craving in the individual. He has to pick out invaluable gems from the bottom of every religion. He can pick up gems only when he approaches religion other than his own with utmost reverance. The moral principles embedded in religion soften human impulses and make him proceed consciously 'Godward.'

If at all theology is attributed to Gandhi, his theology is an alchemy of pragmatism, humanism and rationalism. His religion is pragmatic because he wants that through religion one has to comprehend misery in society, and be able to remove this misery with the help of his religion. When Gandhi said that God satisfies the hungry only when he appears before him with a morsel of food. The conditions of man are to be improved at the same time putting brakes to him, so that he cannot jump into the quagmire of the onrush materialism. Hinduism survived because of its spiritual values in preference to materialism. Gandhi knew that the ancient India is still living. He said: "True, there are dung heaps too here and there (in Hinduism) but there are rich treasures buried under them. And the reason why it (Hinduism) survived is that the end which Hinduism set before it was not development along material but spiritual lives."[4] If religion is not assisting the masses it has no value to Gandhi. Religion should teach the individual to look at others with heart. Compassion and love should dominate him. Only then humanitarian aspect oozes from religion. Gandhi at every stage interpreted religion and its scriptures from this angle. His emphasis was not on religion but on the qualities that have to be inculcated in man. Rationalism is another aspect that was important to Gandhi. In no uncertain terms Gandhi said that nothing is to be accepted as word of God unless it is tested by reason. In his own words: "The scriptures properly so called can only be concerned with eternal virtues and must appeal to any conscience i.e. any heart whose eyes of understanding are opened. Nothing can be accepted as the word of God which cannot be tested by reason or be capable of being spiritually experienced. And even when you have an expurgated edition of the scriptures, you will need their interpretation. Who is the best interpreter? Not learned men, surely learning there must be. But religion does not live by it. It lives in the experience of saints and seers, in their lives and sayings. When all the most learned commentators of the scriptures are utterly forgotten the accumulated experience of the sages and saints will abide and be an inspiration for ages to come."[5] Thus his emphasis was on reason and experience to judge religious sayings.

But when Gandhian theology is looked in isolation without any reference to pragmatism, humanism and rationalism Gandhian vision of religion will not be clear to ordinary mortals. All these shades give different hue and colour to Gandhian religion of ethics. To the majority of the Gandhians, Gandhi was a man of God but not a man of religion. To a critical analyst he is not a man of religion. A penetrating analysis of Gandhi's ethical religion will make clear the reality behind the magnificent radiance that radiates from Gandhi.

Gandhi's was a religion of ethics. God and petitional approach was absent in his view on religion. Ritual and the priest craft have no meaning to him. When all these things are blended, a sort of atheistic streak is visible in his thought. But this atheistic streak in him lies buried in the layers of his thought. The letter and word have to be sifted to recognise the real meaning of the Gandhian writings and declarations. The various aspects of his thought, philosophy, politics, economics, rebelious technique and his pursuasion have to be isolated. These further have to be properly delineated. These are then evaluated. After evaluation these ideas have to be co-related with the events in the historic current. Only then the aim, intention and interpretation by Gandhi will be clear. Interpretation of Gandhi may be accurate only then. At the same time an integrated view of Gandhi has to be evolved.

The liberal thought isolated the individual and made him the centre of study and observation without any reference to any other aspect of society. Liberalism declares that it is not inevitable of history. Man is not at the mercy of fate. He is invincible and infinite in energy to chalk out his progress. He has to be protected from the onslaught of society in case of exploitation from dominant group, ruts of traditional orthodoxy and conservatism. Any attempt to foist man to a predetermined destination robs the gift of freedom from him. Any historical determination, if viewed, puts constraints on the individual. It blurs the vision of man. He will fail to appreciate his endowment of freedom. It is only the freedom that is inherent in man puts him on the journey from the stage of beast to the level of noblest. Application of nonviolence presupposes domination of liberalism. Only the individual thinks in terms of the individual. The principle of nonviolence can be accepted and made the ruling principle in human relations. Any other ideological constraints over the individual other than liberalism makes him ineffective to follow nonviolence in his relations with his fellow beings. The journey to become the noblest was the aim in the teachings of the Buddha, Socrates, Zoroaster and Jesus. They had all tried and infused courage in man to see in him his possession of liberty move as per his conscience. The entire teaching of Gandhi was in this direction. Hold on to the truth and convince the opponent with one's courage to hold on to truth against all odds. Only then the best comes out of him. And this best in him will be vehicle of liberty in him.

The conflict of belief and unbelief is a perpetual conflict. The seers of the *Upanishads*, Mahavira, Buddha, Zoroaster, Socrates, Jesus, Mohammed, Nanak and others taught the masses to go against the traditions they had inherited, and ceremonialism with which they were associated. Because tradition and ceremonialism always stand for the privileged lot in society to perpetuate their interest and domination over the weak. The substance of religion is the blend of love and enlightenment. Once this essence of religion is ignored, fanaticism raises its head resulting into bloodshed. The blood of the weak is shed but not the blood of the dominating few. Thus the inherent unity of mankind is negative. To keep tradition and ritual intact, in a very subtle way the words like faith and wisdom are always brought before credulous. And the vested interests forcefully declare that faith and wisdom transcend reason and intellect. The result was enlightenment as a concept of religion never fully analyzed, nor its benefit to society is never examined fully. Faith and wisdom have a role to play to elevate the individual from misery. As long as faith confined to innate good of man and wisdom when recognises the value of ethics man triumphs over every other thing that conditions him. Gandhi had faith in the divinity of man. His wisdom was that the divinity in man when stirred he is capable of holding on to truth. Holding on to truth is both for the development of the individual and the improvement of his environment.

Growing scientific outlook and spirit accompanied by social conscience keep the man as the centre of society. He is the beginning and end in all calculations. Any deviation from this precept makes the individual weak and becomes an object of exploitation. This concept strips religion of its dogma, its tradition, its ritual and finally its myth. These cannot stand in the way of reason and scientific spirit. In the absence of myth associated with religion, religion is reduced to nothing. When the Marxists proclaim religion is the opium of the masses they are not against the virtues like love and compassion, but against the opiate effect of ceremonies, tradition, ritual and myth associated with religion. These are utilised by the people associated with power to exploit the innocent for their selfish ends. The authorities which get sustenance from religion vehemently condemn the condemnation of the scriptures and the book. Gandhi was fully aware of this. At the same time he knew that religion can be profitably utilized for the uplift of the masses. This would be possible only when ethics is made the basis of religion. The religious inhibitions can be properly devoted to strengthen moral fervour in man. In a very subtle way Gandhi employed religion to make the individual aware of his divinity within.

Very often the votaries of religion insist on a particular behaviour pattern rather than faith in virtues of religion that can be inculcated in the individual. Like the Buddha, Gandhi was also emphatic to accept a thing when reason accepts. Anything contrary to reason is not acceptable. Misery is a part of life. It is natural. Hence one has to suffer. Logic is Good. *Mahants* the custodians of religion preach the same. It is difficult to explain misery in the lives of people. A *mahant* cannot see beyond his selfish ends. Hence exhortation to the masses to suffer misery. On the contrary the seer or the prophet has the vision to eliminate suffering. Remedy is to cultivate virtues, thereby stirring the divinity in man. Gandhi always had faith in divinity in man and strove to subdue evil by divinity. The result will be the mitigation of misery.

The cause of misery of man is his selfishness. In terms of science it is the principle of survival of the fittest. In terms of social sciences man is motivated by economics. Thus selfishness leads to purposive behaviour. Or more clearly it is materialism that stands in the way of refining the individual. Materialism produces greediness and selfishness. Religion that grips man with its ritual and the priest pushes him to a state where he is blind to see divinity in him. Philosophy based on tradition further puts him in darkness. The traditional philosophy educates the individual of pre-determined destination and historical determinism. Both are harmful to creativity in man. At no stage and in no context Gandhi spoke about these two concepts of philosophy. His thrust was to refine man subduing evil in him. The divinity in man was truth to him. And this truth is God to him. In ultimate analysis God is Truth to him.

Religion is always conformist. Supports the established order and the establishment. It supports the authority from where it gets sustenance. Religion is never a social reform movement. Religion gets reformed by the impact of social necessity and man's reason. If religion is truth, truth does not require reform. Love and compassion do not require reform. Virtues do not require reform. Religion is not a virtue hence reform is essential.

To make religion acceptable, votaries of religion and the supporters of contemporary social edifice attribute virtues in man to religion. Gandhi, a rebel and a revolutionary asked his audience to look for good. He tried to restructure the individual to be fit to march on his path to the noblest. He was not at all frightened to be called himself a super atheist, when his acts so warranted. He was an action oriented leader. In his scheme of things if religion is a stumbling block he would have not only removed it but would have thrown it over board. Religion came to him handy to convey his message. He employed theistic medium and idiom. Therefore to the Gandhians he was a man of God. A slight obliteration of religion is sacrilege to them. On the contrary Gandhi labelled himself a super atheist if this helped him to further his scheme of things.

REFERENCES

1. Jawaharlal Nehru, *Mahatma Gandhi*, Asia Publishing House, 1949, p. 19.
2. *Young India*, 8 April, 1926.
3. *Ibid.*
4. *Young India*, 24 November, 1927.
5. *Harijan*, 18 July, 1936.

BIBLIOGRAPHY

Dave, J. H. : *Immortal India*; Vol. I, Bharatiya Vidya Bhavan, Bombay, 1957.

Gandhi, M. K. : *An Autobiography*; 'The story of my Experiments with truth' Navajeevan Publishing House : Ahmedabad, 1951.

Gandhi, M. K. : *Hind Swaraj* : Navajeevan Publishing House, Ahmedabad, 1951.

Gandhi, M. K. : *From Yerwade Mandi* : English Translation Navajeevan Publishing House, Ahmedabad.

Gandhi, M. K. : *Prayer* : Navajeevan Publishing House, Ahmedabad, 1955.

Gandhi, M. K. : *Ashram Observance in Action* : Navajeevan Publishing House, Ahmedabad, 1955.

Gandhi, M. K. : *Hindu Dharma* : Navajeevan Publishing House, Ahmedabad, 1950.

Gandhi, M. K. : *Satyagraha in South Africa* : Navajeevan Publishing House, Ahmedabad, 1950.

Gandhi, M. K. : *In Search of the Supreme*, Vols. I, II, III. Navajeevan Publishing House, Ahmedabad, 1961, 1962.

Gandhi, M. K. : *My Religion* : Navajeevan Publishing House, Ahmedabad, Reprints 1984.

Gandhi, M. K. ; *Khadi* : Navajeevan Publishing House, Ahmedabad.

Gora : *An Atheist with Gandhi*; Navajeevan Publishing House, Ahmedabad, 1951.

Iwar, Topa : *Ethics of Non-violence* : Navajeevan Publishing House, Ahmedabad, 1964.

Iyer, Raghavan : *The Moral and Political Writing of Mahatma Gandhi* : Clarendon Press Oxford, 1986.

John, Levy : *Immediate Knowledge and Happiness* : Thorsons Publishers, London, 1970.

Joseph, J. Dorce : *M. K. Gandhi : An Indian Patriot in South Africa* : Publications Divisions, New Delhi,1967.

Kalidas Nag : *Tolstoy and Gandhi* : Pustak Bhandar, Patna 1950.

Singh : *In Search of Religion* : Vision Books Pvt Ltd., New 1978.

Karve, Iravati : *Yugantar* (The End of an Epoch) Sangam Books, New Delhi, 1974.

Krishnadas : *Seven Months with Mahatma Gandhi* : Navajeevan Publishing House, Ahmedabad, 1961.

Nehru, Jawaharlal : *Mahatma Gandhi*, Asia Publishing House, 1949, *A Bunch of Old Letters*.

Periodicals : *Young India*, Harijan.

Ranade, R. D. : *The Conception of Spiritual Life in Mahatma and Hindu Saints*; Gujarat Vidyasabha, Ahmedabad, 1956.

A Readers Digest Publication 1984 : *The Great People of Faith and Wisdom*.

Index

To Gandhi religion means the principle enunciated in the Sermon on the Mount with the elucidation from the *Gita*. In the light of this Ishopanishad of the *Upanishads* has to be understood and practised in structuring the man, so that the principle of *Ahimsa* becomes the operative formula and makes the individual a true *Satyagrahi* not merely for political purposes but helps towards the movement of society. The three things which Gandhi valued in *Ishopanishad* are: 'Renounce it and enjoy it. Enjoy what He gives you. Do not covet any body's wealth or possession.'

"This *Mantra* has to be understood in the light of the teachings in the *Gita*. Similarly the *Gita* has to be understood in the light of this *Mantra* of *Ishopanishad*." Further Gandhi felt that this *Mantra* satisfies the cravings of a socialist, a communist, a philosopher and an economist. Again it also caters to the thinking of those who do not belong to Hindu fold.

From this angle the [illegible] *Dharma* which the Gandhians associated with Gandhi's idea of religion is framed and identified with the word religion. The words religion and *Dharma* are viewed as similar to each other. The result was that Gandhi was interpreted in religious terms as understood in the common parlance. Taking an overview of the Gandhian ideas and his political aim one could see that the word *Dharma* leans not on religion as understood but on obligations—obligations towards fellowmen, towards one's own group, the state and society. [illegible] further analysed what this word *Dharma* meant is that it denotes an inbuilt input in Gandhian society to soften and to remove friction between social groups on one hand and on the other the individual and society. This ultimately culminates into the establishment of a frictionless society and gradually wiping out exploitation. The medium through which it is possible is to operate the principle of *Ahimsa*. The aim of frictionless society is *Sarvodaya*. This does not mean an evolutionary process. At every stage Gandhi was for revolution. He was a reformer vis-a-vis a freedom fighter. He was always in a hurry. Only limitation was *Ahimsa*.

Gandhi's ideas on religion attracted the common masses as well as the Indian intellectuals, [illegible] both in the [illegible] and the [illegible].

The [illegible] man was [illegible] in [illegible] [illegible] *Dharma* [illegible] protection [illegible]